Gordon Ramsay

CELEBRITY
CHEFS

Gordon
Ramsay

Jeanne Nagle

Enslow Publishing
101 W. 23rd Street
Suite 240
New York, NY 10011
USA

enslow.com

Published in 2016 by Enslow Publishing, LLC
101 W. 23rd Street, Suite 240, New York, NY 10011

Library of Congress Cataloging-in-Publication Data

Names: Nagle, Jeanne.
Title: Gordon Ramsay / Jeanne Nagle.
Description: First edition. | New York, NY : Enslow Publishing, 2016. |
  Series: Celebrity chefs | Audience: Grades 6 to 12. | Includes
  bibliographical references and index.
Identifiers: LCCN 2015036138| ISBN 9780766072466 (library bound) | ISBN
Subjects: LCSH: Ramsay, Gordon--Juvenile literature. | Cooks--Great
  Britain--Biography--Juvenile literature. | Celebrity chefs--Great
  Britain--Biography--Juvenile literature.
Classification: LCC TX649.R26 N34 2016 | DDC 641.5092--dc23
LC record available at http://lccn.loc.gov/2015036138

Printed in the United States of America

To Our Readers: We have done our best to make sure all website addresses in this book were active and appropriate when we went to press. However, the author and the publisher have no control over and assume no liability for the material available on those websites or on any websites they may link to. Any comments or suggestions can be sent by e-mail to customerservice@enslow.com.

Photo Credits: Cover, p. 3, 6, 32 Ethan Miller/Getty Images for Vegas Uncork'd by Bon Appetit/Getty Images; p. 9 Bryan Steffy/Getty Images North America/Getty Images; pp. 12, 29, 42, 70, 82 Dave Benett/Hulton Archive/Getty Images; p. 14 Matthew Lewis/Getty Images Entertainment/Getty Images; pp. 18, 72 Fuse/Thinkstock; p. 24 © Pawel Libera Images/ Alamy Stock Photo; p. 26 Christopher Pillitz/Hulton Archive/Getty Images; p. 34 Patrick Riviere/Getty Images Entertainment/Getty Images; p. 39 Ken Towner / Evening Standard/ Rex/REX USA; p. 45 Karwai Tang/WireImage/Getty Images; pp. 47, 105 GERRY PENNY/ AFP/Getty Images; p. 50 Steve Parsons/PA Wire/AP Images; p. 57 © 20th Century Fox Film Corp. All rights reserved./courtesy Everett Collection; p. 59 Anthony Harvey/Getty Images Entertainment/Getty Images; p. 63 © 20th Century Fox Film Corp. All rights reserved./ courtesy Everett Collection; p. 64 Greg Gayne /© Fox / courtesy Everett Collection; p. 66 Rex Features via AP Images; p. 75 Ethan Miller/Getty Images Entertainment/Thinkstock; p. 76 Rick Madonik/Toronto Star/Getty Images; p. 78 Mike Floyd/Rex/REX USA; p. 84 DANNY LAWSON/PA Photos /Landov; p. 87 Dave Hogan/Getty Images Entertainment/Getty Images; p. 88 Nigel Roddis/Getty Images Sport/Getty Images for Ironman; p. 90 Phil Walter/Getty Images News/Getty Images; p. 94 Klaus Vedfelt/Iconica/Getty Images; p. 96 wavebreakmedia/ Shutterstock.com; p. 99 monkeybusinessimages/iStock/Thinkstock; . 102 FOOD AND DRINK PHOTOS/Food and Drink/SuperStock; p. 109 Oksana Shufrych/shutterstock.com; p. 110 iStock.com/margouillatphotos; p. 112 rodrigobark/iStock/Thinkstock; p. 115 iStock. com/JackJelly; p. 117 © FoodCollection/age fotostock; p. 119 vikif/iStock/Thinkstock; p. 121 tycoon751/iStock/Thinkstock; p. 124 bhofack2/iStock/Thinkstock; p. 126 graletta/ Shutterstock.com; p. 129 Aleksandrova Karina/Shutterstock.com.

CONTENTS

Gordon Ramsay has used his talents as a master chef to feed, entertain, and lend assistance to people all around the world.

Chapter

1

A Spicy
Childhood

It may seem like Chef Gordon Ramsay is everywhere. His face stares out from the pages of his cookbooks that grace store shelves, and he is something of a fixture on television in the United States and, especially, Britain. Ramsay owns or has a stake in twenty-five restaurants—and counting—in multiple cities across four continents. Ramsay's perceived omnipresence, meaning the ability to be everywhere all the time, is not an accident. It is actually a clever marketing maneuver that uses Ramsay's natural passion and energy to help sell his product—himself.

So far, the plan seems to be working pretty well. Forbes magazine estimated that Ramsay earned $60 million in 2015.[1] Various sources put his net worth, meaning the value of everything he owns minus any debts owed, at anywhere between $140 million and $175 million.[2] More than the money, Ramsay enjoys a celebrity status that is usually reserved for rock stars, sports legends, and A-list Hollywood actors. Granted, some people would argue that he is most well known for his hot temper and frequently obscene language. But in fact he is admired for his talent as a chef and respected for his ambition to be the best at anything he attempts. "Work is who I am, who I want to be," Ramsay admitted in his 2006 autobiography. "I sometimes think that if I were to stop, I'd cease to exist."[3]

Growing Up The Hard Way

Gordon James Ramsay was born in Renfrewshire, Scotland on November 8, 1966. He was the second of four children, two boys and two girls. His sister Diane is the eldest, and brother Ronnie and sister Yvonne were born after Gordon. His mother, Helen, was trained as a nurse, but she worked a variety of unrelated jobs when Gordon was young. Among these were working at a newsagent's shop, what Americans would call a newsstand, and as a waitress in a cafe. Later she would work steadily in various nursing homes.

His father, also named Gordon, worked sometimes as a welder, sometimes as a pool manager. The latter was a natural fit for Gordon senior, who swam competitively at the national level in Scotland as a teenager. Being a competitive athlete was a trait that never seemed to leave him, and it was a trait he appeared to have passed on to his first-born son. Young Gordon used to run along the length of the pool while his father swam alongside, seeing who was faster.

The senior Gordon drank quite a bit and had a hot temper. When he was drunk he could be abusive toward his wife and children. These episodes stemmed from the fact that he was unhappy with his lot in life. His dream was to be a professional musician, and he played and sang in various bands but never seemed to find success, much less a recording contract.

Growing up in a working-class Scottish family with no special love for cooking, there were no hints that Ramsay would be the star chef he is today.

Chip Off the ★ Old Block?

Anyone who has seen Chef Ramsay in action might suspect that he got his temper and competitiveness from his father. While that may be true, Gordon says he was the exact opposite as a child. "Until I was big enough to take [my father] on in a fight, I wouldn't have said 'boo' to a goose."[4]

He believes he is more like his mother, whom he admires for the way in which she handled herself all those years in an abusive marriage. "I have her strength," he wrote in his autobiography, "... the ability to keep going no matter what life throws at you."[5] He does note a major difference between his cooking style and that of his mother, who worked in the kitchen of a teashop. "It amazes me today how she just got on with it and never cursed."[6]

The family moved around quite a bit, going back and forth from Scotland to England every time Gordon senior needed to find work. Unfortunately, he was often out of work. The younger Gordon Ramsay has described his father as "gobby," which means he was opinionated, loud, and disrespectful. He talked back to his bosses, and got fired as a result. His frequent unemployment meant the Ramsays did not have much money. Most often they lived in council estate, or government-supported, housing. Nearly everything they owned was bought used or on a payment plan.

Mealtime at the Ramsay Home

Young Gordon did not grow up eating the type of food he would go on to prepare as an adult chef. In fact, the very idea of having a full, sit-down meal with appetizers or a salad, a main course, and dessert was a totally foreign idea to him and his family. Instead, they would eat simple meals, prepared by his mother from whatever ingredients she had on hand or could afford to buy. Helen Ramsay prepared homemade fish and chips, a traditional English dish that Gordon likes to this day. When they had meat, it was usually less expensive sausages and chops, rather than prime cuts such as steak. Eggs also were an affordable staple in the household, but fruit was a rare treat. When a loaf of bread got stale, she whipped up an easy, and cheap, dessert called bread and butter pudding.

Gordon's mother also created meals out of bits and parts that were left over from various animals that had been butchered, called offal. From ham hocks, which are basically pig ankles, she made the broth that was the base of a hearty soup. Everybody's least favorite dinner in the Ramsay house was tripe, which is the lining of a cow's stomach. His mother cooked

Helen Ramsay cooked the best meals she could on a limited budget. While Gordon didn't learn techniques or recipes from her, he did absorb the importance of creativity in the kitchen.

it in milk with onions.[7] When the family had porridge, such as oatmeal, his father would all but ruin it by over-salting young Gordon's portion. He claimed it would make a man out of the lad.[8]

The Ramsay children were taught not to waste food, and to eat everything that was set before them. "I laugh when I see people playing with food," he told an interviewer in 2014. Such an act would not have been tolerated in the Ramsay house. "God Almighty, you'd get clipped around the ear!"[9]

First Choice of Career

Many young boys in the United Kingdom (England, Scotland, Wales, and Northern Ireland) have grown up dreaming of being a professional footballer, known as a soccer player in the United States. Young Gordon Ramsay was no exception. Yet he had an extra reason to work toward becoming a professional athlete—pleasing his former-athlete father. His ultimate goal was to play for the Glasgow Rangers, his father's favorite team.

Gordon discovered that he was pretty good at the game while playing for his school team. When he was sixteen and ready to leave high school (secondary education ends at age sixteen in the United Kingdom), he earned a spot with the semi-professional team in Banbury, where he was staying with his older sister Diane in a rented flat, or apartment. (He had left home after having had a tremendous fight with his father.) Around this time a scout for the Rangers saw him playing in a Football Association youth league (eighteen and under) game and invited him to spend a week during the summer training with the team in Glasgow. He jumped at the chance at what amounted to a tryout with the Rangers.

While Ramsay didn't reach his dream goal of becoming a professional football (soccer) star, his fame as a chef has allowed him to play in charity events.

Apparently the team liked what they saw because they called him back up to Glasgow for training, so he could work for a contract and a spot on the reserve team. The reserve team is basically a second-string squad made up of players who are new to the pro game or first-team players who are coming back from an injury. One minor catch was that Gordon would have to leave the Banbury apartment and move back in with his parents, who were living in Glasgow at the time. The team also required that sixteen-year-old Gordon have his father accompany him to training. It was not an ideal situation, one that put a lot of pressure on him, but he managed as best he could for the sake of his future in professional sports. While he was not under contract and he wouldn't see much playing time during games, Gordon had essentially made it to the big time.

Unfortunately, his football career was short-lived. He was with the team for a little more than a year, and had played in a few reserve-team games and friendlies, which are like exhibition games, when he was injured during training. The cartilage in his knee was damaged, resulting in his being out for eleven weeks. Shortly after he had recovered he reinjured the knee while playing a game of squash, tearing a ligament and being placed in a cast for a month. Coming back from the second injury, at least as far as playing professionally went, proved to be a nonstarter. His time with the Rangers had come to an end.

Refuge in the Kitchen

Although he was terribly disappointed that he would no longer be playing professional football, Gordon had a back-up plan in place. Because he had only passed two of his "O-levels," which were course-specific exams that showed how well a student did in high school, he had not qualified to directly enter college.

Beefing Up His
★ Football Resume

For years Ramsay had maintained that he played two games for the Rangers on the first team, which was made up of starters and star players. That declaration was later proved to be false. Representatives from the Rangers organization have stated that their records show that Ramsay played as a trialist, meaning someone who was trying out for the team, but was never on the first team. In 2009, Ramsay admitted he had made what his spokesperson called an "inaccurate" claim.

Instead, he took what is known as foundation, or bridge, courses in the culinary arts at the North Oxfordshire Technical College in Banbury.

He had enrolled at the school before trying out for the Rangers. Officially Gordon studied hotel management, but his real interest was in catering, or working as a chef. Journalist Neil Simpson claims that seeing what went on behind the scenes in the kitchen of a teashop, or cafe, where his mother had been working is what first piqued his interest in being a chef. He goes on to state that Gordon enrolled at North Oxfordshire because everyone working together in controlled chaos reminded him of being on a football team, which, at the time, was what he had planned to do for a living. Working in a kitchen would be a suitable alternative to playing football.[10] In his later years, Gordon would remember the situation a bit differently. Rather than being a secondary dream come true, he viewed taking culinary classes as "an accident, a complete accident."[11]

> *"I think cooking is a lot like football. It's not a job, it's a passion."*

His father, on the other hand, viewed Gordon attending culinary school and becoming a chef as a huge mistake. Gordon senior believed that cooking was a woman's job, and that any man who did so was not very masculine.

By this time Gordon was back living with Diane in Banbury. He did not have enough money to afford the chef's whites—the outfit worn by professional chefs—or other materials such as a set of professional knives. A local civic group, the Round Table, provided the funds to get him whatever he needed to stay in school. He recalls how proud he was to have those whites and

Ramsay finally found the success he was looking for when he fell into cooking. Studying the culinary arts and getting his first taste of working in professional kitchens sparked in him the need to succeed.

knives, treating them with the same love and care as he did his beloved boots when he was playing football.[12]

In his autobiography, Gordon states that he greatly enjoyed the energy of a busy eatery. One of the weekend jobs he held while attending classes was washing dishes at a curry house in Stratford. "I was in the kitchen, listening to all the noise, and I was fascinated. I couldn't believe the way people were shouting at each other. ... I was enraptured."[13]

As failing many of his O-level exams attests, Gordon was not a prize student. He managed to turn that around, though, at North Oxfordshire. Bound and determined to become the best chef he possibly could be he threw himself into his studies. "Now the football had ended I knew that I couldn't afford to mess up a second time," he has said. "I was obsessed with never again being told that I'm not good enough. I had failed once in life. I swore I would never fail at anything ever again."[14]

Chapter 2

Hungry for
Experience

Gordon Ramsay would be the first to admit that he did not start out as a master chef right from the get-go. Some of the early dishes he attempted kind of went off the rails a bit. For instance, Ramsay tells an amusing story about how he once accidentally substituted dishwashing liquid for vinegar in a sauce he was concocting.[1] But the chef-in-training did not let such troubles get him down for long. Even though he had promised himself that he would be an excellent chef one day, he knew he had to study hard and learn how to make that happen. "I pushed myself beyond belief," he writes in his autobiography. "I was happy to learn the basics. I didn't find it demeaning at all."[2]

After Ramsay had completed a year at North Oxfordshire, one of his teachers suggested that he work in a kitchen full-time and attend college on a part-time basis. Ramsay believed that if the teacher thought he was ready, then he should be willing to give it a try. Thus, he went from full-time college student and part-time dishwasher to part-time student and full-time working chef.

Now We're Cooking!

Ramsay did not have to look to far to find his first chef job; he took a position in the kitchen of the Roxburgh House Hotel in Banbury, where he had been working part time as a dishwasher. Even though he was already an employee and he had taken college courses in cooking and hotel management, he did not start out as a full-fledged chef. His title was commis chef. Commis chefs are beginners who help out wherever they can.

At Roxbrough, he worked under a head chef named Andy Rogers, who, as Ramsay recalled years later, mostly taught him how *not* to prepare food. Apparently everything that came out of the kitchen was fried and stuffed with cheese. Worse yet, in Ramsay's estimation, many ingredients were not fresh, but originated in a can. "I saw so many shortcuts done badly," he later told a reporter about his experiences in the hotel kitchen.[3] When he tried to share some of the tricks and secrets he had been taught in culinary school, Chef Rogers would yell at him and basically tell Ramsay that he could stuff his education and the cooking methods the school had taught him. That type of treatment must have reinforced a lesson anyone who wants to work in a professional kitchen should learn—the head chef runs the show.

> *Sources report that Gordon received his Higher National Degree (HND) in hotel management in 1987.*

★ On the Job Training

Being a commis, or junior, chef allows aspiring cooks to learn the tricks of the trade from more experienced members of the staff. Professional kitchens are divided into several sections, and commis chefs are expected to develop their skills by watching and participating, in order to become proficient at each station.

To better understand what a commis chef does, one need only check out the qualifications listed in a job posting from one of Ramsay's own restaurants. The candidate needs to learn and understand all the dishes on the menu. He or she helps prepare ingredients by performing tasks such as washing and chopping produce. Adhering to the kitchen cleaning schedule and following food safety requirements are essential. Above all, the commis chef must follow instructions given by senior chefs and deliver what is requested of him or her in a timely manner.

After six months, Ramsay moved on from Roxbrough House to a sixty-seat village restaurant called the Wickham Arms. By his account, he was in charge of the entire kitchen and dining room, despite only having six months as a commis chef under his belt. Essentially he was the head chef. This gave Ramsay the opportunity to spread his culinary wings in a relatively low-stakes setting. The restaurant's menu included hare and venison, as well as dishes he had read about in cookbooks.

Ramsay enjoyed the freedom of running his own kitchen at Wickham Arms. Yet he realized that he was never going to become the kind of chef he wanted to be by staying in Oxfordshire. So in 1986 he packed his bags and his knives and headed off to find work in the kitchens of London.

London Calling

Ramsay knew that he would essentially be starting over by going to the big city. Although his time at Wickham Arms was a good experience that boosted his confidence in his abilities, the village establishment was not in the same league as the posh restaurants of London. His experience working in a professional kitchen did give him a miniscule advantage, however. When he landed a job at London's Mayfair Hotel, he was automatically made a second, or grade two, commis. That was a step above being a commis at Roxbrough House, although it also was a step down from acting as head chef at Wickham Arms.

Ramsay did not care much about his title. He was happy to be working in the kitchen of a luxury hotel in the largest city in the United Kingdom. He was part of the team that cooked for customers in the banquet hall and fulfilled room-service orders. On occasion he even got to work with the French staff of the hotel's fine-dining restaurant. The French have an excellent

For a young chef like Ramsay, London was the place to be. He quickly secured employment at luxury hotel Mayfair, where he prepared food for hotel banquets and room service orders.

culinary reputation, so working with them was something of a treat for the young chef. Apparently they could also be a little tough on their fellow workers. Anyone who messed up during the service of a meal was sent away from fine dining to work in the hotel's coffee shop.[4]

Working for a Dictator

After sixteen months, Ramsay decided to leave the Mayfair. While working at a restaurant in Soho, Brazanga, he came upon an article about Marco Pierre White, the head chef and owner of Harvey's. White was a celebrity chef before there officially were celebrity chefs. He was, and still is, known as much for his odd-to-bad behavior as he is for his food. White trained with a number of French chefs, including brothers Albert and Michel Roux. The public may also have been fascinated with White because he was very young for such an accomplished chef. He was only five years older than Ramsay, who approached White in 1988, looking for a job.

According to the account in his autobiography, Ramsay basically auditioned for White by making ravioli and tortellini, something he had never attempted before. White dismissed Ramsay's efforts as imperfect and not worthy of being served to customers. However, he did like how quickly Ramsay had worked, and offered him a job on the spot. Ramsay had to give notice to his current employer, but he did not want to lose the opportunity of working with White. So he wound up spending all day in Brazanga's kitchen, then commuting to work at Harvey's until 2 a.m.—for an entire month.

If Ramsay had not learned his lesson about the head chef being in charge before, he certainly did while working under White. "Marco was running a dictatorship: his word, and his

Ramsay moved on to work with Marco Pierre White (right) at the trendy restaurant Harvey's. Like Ramsay's father, White could be cruel and abusive towards his staff. Still, Ramsay credits White with making him the chef he is today.

word alone, was all that mattered," he later wrote.[5] Tales of White throwing pans of food, insulting and humiliating his staff, and even being physically abusive were legendary. His moods changed at the drop of a hat. One minute everything would be fine, then the next a pot of sauce would go flying across the kitchen.

But White was also a brilliant and talented chef. He was credited with breathing new life into the British culinary scene at the time. His staff put up with the abuse because they learned so much from their head chef. Ramsay admired not only White's strong work ethic—which he expected his staff to mirror—but also the fresh, made-to-order quality of the dishes he created. White shared his technique with Ramsay, who, years later, would incorporate many of those qualities in his own cooking. "Lightness, delicacy, finesse, balance—I wouldn't be where I am now if it weren't for Marco," he was quoted as saying in a 2007 *New Yorker* article.[7]

> *"Kitchens are hard environments and they form incredibly strong characters."*[6]

Ramsay believes that growing up with an abusive father helped prepare him to deal with White, and stick it out in a difficult situation. He rose from his start as a commis to being Harvey's sous chef, which made him second in command. In fact, there were times when Ramsay was actually running the restaurant's kitchen on his own.

As one might suspect, kitchen turnover was high at Harvey's during the nearly three years that Ramsay worked there. In addition to White's rages, staff had to contend with the long hours and lack of personal time that tend to be part and parcel of working as a chef at that level. Ramsay had walked out before, reportedly after White threatened to fire him for not kicking his roommate, a former Harvey's kitchen staffer, out of their apartment. But White managed to get him back in the kitchen.

Commis Again?

Eventually, though, Ramsay grew tired of the tension and exhaustion. More than that, he wanted to work in France, which is the goal of many an aspiring chef. White convinced him that he should work at a French restaurant in England first, and got him an interview with Frenchman Albert Roux, who ran the kitchen at Le Gavroche. Essentially, working at Gavroche would be a kind of "test drive" for actually working in France.

Starting over at a new restaurant came at a price, he was hired as a commis, which meant he was making less money than he had been at Harvey's. In order to help make ends meet, he picked up a couple of shifts at Harvey's on the side. When Le Gavroche management discovered his moonlighting, Ramsay made a complete break from Harvey's, and White. After an initial bout of anger, Albert's son, Michel, turned out to be sympathetic to his situation. He lent Ramsay some money so the young chef could pay off some debts.

More than a year after joining the staff of Le Gavroche Ramsay was asked to work a fifteen-week season with Chef Roux at Hotel Diva, a resort in the French Alps where Roux was a consultant. Not only was it an incredible honor for Ramsay to be asked, but the move enabled him to realize his dream of cooking in France. While there he also learned to speak French— he had used a translator in the Gavroche kitchen—immersed himself in French culture, and even got in a little skiing.

When Ramsay took a pay cut to work for Albert Roux at French restaurant Le Gavroche, Roux's son Michel (celebrating here with Ramsay) helped him make ends meet. Michelin two-star chef Michel Roux has since taken over the family business.

Quite the
★Transformation

On the occasion of fortieth anniversary of Le Gavroche opening its doors, Michel Roux the younger—his famous-chef uncle also is named Michel—reminisced about Ramsay's time in the restaurant's kitchen. Roux described what appears to be a transformation, a kind of "worst to first" story:

> Gordon's first week was probably one of the worst weeks of his life. He was probably the most untidy, clumsy chef that ever walked into our kitchens. He was all over the place. And mucky, dirty. Now look at him. He is spotless, organized, switched on. I can honestly say that he has been the most talented chef I have seen in the Gavroche kitchens.[8]

On to Paris

After his short stay at Diva, Ramsay traveled on to Paris, with the blessings of, and recommendations from, the Rouxs. In the French capital he landed a job at Guy Savoy, which was named after its head chef and owner. During the first few months of his time at the restaurant he worked at the pastry station, which was located in a level of the building below the main kitchen. Because he knew he could do so much more than make delicious sorbets and fruit tarts, Ramsay made it his goal to move to the upstairs kitchen.

A couple of roadblocks stood in his way, not the least of which was that the French chefs and staff considered him an English intruder. They made sure to put him through his paces and keep him in what they thought should be his place. For example, the pastry chef, whom Ramsay remembers as "a little squirt" of a man, enjoyed overseeing as Ramsay performed dull, routine tasks such as sharpening knives and sweeping the floor. Ramsay was also expected to bring the man's meals and coffee to him. "If he was trying to break me—well, the bigger [jerk] he was to me, the more it helped me keep going," Ramsay has written.[9]

Eventually he made his way upstairs, to the fish station of the main kitchen. Ramsay arrived early, stayed late, and kept his eyes wide open while observing how the restaurant was run. His work ethic and eagerness to learn earned him the respect of Chef Savoy. After a year on the job, Savoy offered Ramsay the position of being his second-in-command. While he liked and admired Savoy, Ramsay declined the offer. He felt being a number two, even at such a renowned establishment such as Guy Savoy, would hold him back. So off he went, in search of another job.

Once in Paris, an essential experience for many chefs, Ramsay worked for Chef Guy Savoy at his namesake restaurant. At the prestigious eatery, Ramsay eagerly learned all he could, dazzling Chef Savoy enough to be offered a coveted position.

Savoy had recommended him to another Parisian restauranteur named Joel Robuchon, who ran a highly regarded restaurant that bore his name. Back to being a commis again, Ramsay found himself in a situation similar to what he had gone through at Harvey's. Apparently, Chef Robuchon had a temper to match that of Marco Pierre White. The hours were long and the breaks were nonexistent. Ramsay once likened working there to being in a special military unit. Additionally, it was hard to climb the career ladder at the restaurant, especially for an outsider Brit like Ramsay. This was not the change that he had hoped he would find when he left Guy Savoy. He only stayed at Robuchon for ten months.

Getting Onboard

Once he had given notice that he was leaving, Ramsay landed a job that he considered part adventure, part vacation. He signed on to be the chef aboard the yacht of Australian millionaire Reg Grundy and his actress wife, Joy Chambers. The salary was decent, and the tips were supposed to add greatly to someone's income. Ramsay's goal was to save money so that he could eventually open his own restaurant.

At first working on the boat was a dream come true. The kitchen of the *Idlewild*, which was what the yacht was named, was modern and relatively large for a ship. Ramsay was the head chef, which meant he cooked for the owners and their guests when they were aboard. (Grundy and Chambers were on the boat only for a handful of weeks at a time.) The lowly chore of feeding the crew went to his assistant.

Cooking for the couple was a joy. They were health conscious, so they wanted fine cuisine that was on the lighter side. Ramsay has said that his current style of cooking, with an emphasis on

With the singular goal of earning enough money to finance the opening of his own restaurant, Ramsay turned to the private sector, serving as head chef on the yacht of wealthy Australians Reg Grundy and Joy Chambers.

eating well but healthily, was greatly influenced by his time on the ship.

During his free time Ramsay could be found diving, water-skiing or fishing off the prow (front) of the yacht. But even paradise can get tiring after a while. Besides, Ramsay was eager to get back to dry land and open his own restaurant. After nine months traveling around Europe and the Caribbean, he bid the ship and its owners farewell, took his savings, and headed back to London.

An Assist
⭐ From Mum

While Ramsay was at sea on the *Idlewild*, Chambers had a craving for Shepherd's pie. This is an English dish traditionally made of ground lamb and vegetables in a brown sauce, with a mashed-potato topping. The only trouble was that, despite being a chef and a native of the United Kingdom, Ramsay had no idea how to make it. So he got on the yacht's ship-to-shore phone and called the one cook he knew he could rely on in a pinch such as this—his mother. Following her recipe, he presented the Grundy and Chambers with a beautiful shepherd's pie at dinner, for which he won rave reviews.

Chapter
3

Calling the
Shots

Despite his intention to be the head chef of his own restaurant, Ramsay wound up going in a different direction when he arrived back in London ... at least temporarily. Celebrated French-born chef Pierre Koffmann was looking for a new head chef for his restaurant La Tante Claire. He offered Ramsay the job. Since it was such an impressive position at the time, Ramsay said yes.

Trouble started soon after he started work. It was nice being the head chef, and he earned a good paycheck. Yet Ramsay felt as if he was being held back. He and Koffmann frequently had disagreements about what special dishes should go on the menu. Koffmann, being the owner, almost always go his way. What good was being a head chef if Ramsay could not even create his own menu?

Ramsay's frustration was alive and well when he got a call from Marco Pierre White, his former boss at Harvey's. White wanted to discuss a business deal. The Rossmore, a failing restaurant in the Chelsea district owned by a business partner of White's, was in need of help. White offered Ramsay an ownership share—some sources say 10 percent while others, including Ramsay in his autobiography, say 25 percent—in the establishment. The majority shareholders, who put up the money to open the restaurant and owned a larger percentage of the place, belonged to a group called A-Z Restaurants. White would have no share in the restaurant and no say in the way it was run.

Ramsay had only been at La Tante Claire for three months, but he felt he knew what he had to do. He accepted the deal. He was twenty-six years old, and he finally had an ownership stake in a place of his own.

Welcome to Aubergine

Ramsay had to pull things together quickly to open the newly renamed Aubergine as planned on Oct. 1, 1993. That included painting the restaurant walls, which Ramsay claims to have done himself. He chose to offer eight entrees on a menu that changed every three months. His signature move was to take simple ingredients and make them something special. For instance, he would "dress up" inexpensive meat or fish with flavorful, inventive sauces and unusual sides, such as the root vegetable, salsify.[1]

Restaurants, and their chefs, depend on getting good reviews to attract customers and keep them in business. Fairly glowing reviews and positive word of mouth made Aubergine a success soon after its opening. In just a little over a year, the restaurant received one of the best reviews it could hope to get. Chef Ramsay's cuisine and the service at Aubergine earned their first star from the world-famous Michelin Guide. In the restaurant business, Michelin stars are an honor reserved only

Ramsay finally realized his dream when he opened Aubergine in 1993. With an ownership stake and control over the menu and the running of the restaurant, Ramsay was able to put his signature on the restaurant. Under Ramsay's leadership, Aubergine earned two Michelin stars within a few short years.

★ Seeing Stars

First published in 1900, the Michelin Guide was an attempt to lead motor travelers to helpful locations such as hotels and gas stations. The guide first began awarding stars to restaurants in France in 1926. Coverage has since expanded to include several cities throughout Europe, the United States, and parts of Asia. Reviews are conducted anonymously. The one-to-three-star rating system offers recommendations, as follows:

One star:
"A very good restaurant in its category"

Two stars:
"Excellent cooking, worth a detour"

Three stars:
"Exceptional cuisine, worth a special journey"

Technically, Michelin stars are awarded to, and kept by, chefs, not the restaurants at which they work. Fans of fine dining place a great deal of importance on the Michelin ratings. Not winning stars, or losing stars at subsequent reviews, can cause a restaurant to lose business.

for the finest and best restaurants. They are the equivalent of a seal of approval, or a badge of honor.

Ramsay was thrilled when he was awarded his first star. In a way it justified all his hard work and all the obstacles he had gone through to become a chef. Yet he was not completely satisfied. After all, there were more stars that could be earned. Two years later, the Michelin Guide awarded a second star to Aubergine. Ramsay was happy because the only other restaurant that had earned two stars in so short a time was Harvey's. Of course, he still had not reached his ultimate goal, which was earning three stars.

An Offer Refused

Running the kitchen as part owner of Aubergine kept Ramsay plenty busy. But in 1995, Marco Pierre White upped the ante by making him an incredible offer. White was offering to pay Ramsay an obscene amount of money to come work with him and be his "best of chefs."[2] Ramsay politely refused the offer, because he wanted to work toward earning three stars on his own, not as a part of White's team. Angered by what he felt was an insult from Ramsay, White revealed that the other owners of Aubergine were in debt, and that they were going to sell the restaurant out from under Ramsay.

Ramsay talked to the other shareholders at A-Z Restaurants, who assured him that although there were some money issues, they were no plans to close Aubergine. In fact, they had decided to open another fine-dining restaurant. They offered Ramsay a share in the new restaurant as well, in exchange for him finding them a qualified chef to run the place. Ramsay tapped his friend, and former sous chef at Aubergine, Marcus

The firing of Ramsay's friend Marcus Wareing (right) was the final straw in a series of betrayals and questionable business dealings. However, this motivated Ramsay to open his own place.

Wareing for the head chef position at what became L'Oranger. The new restaurant opened in 1996.

That same year, Ramsay married Cayetana Hutcheson, who was known as Tana. He met her when she and her former fiancé, another chef, were dining at Aubergine.

Leading a Revolt

Aubergine continued to draw crowds and appeared to be doing well, as was L'Oranger. Yet Ramsay still had an uneasy feeling about his business partners—as it turns out, with good reason. A series of shady and confusing business deals conducted by A-Z Restaurants left Ramsay essentially powerless as an owner of Aubergine. He also was stripped of power as a consulting manager of the other restaurant he had a share in, L'Oranger. When the head chef at L'Oranger, Ramsay's friend Marcus Wareing, was fired without his approval, Ramsay had had enough. During the prior six months he had secretly been working on a deal that would have him opening a new restaurant at the former site of his old workplace La Tante Claire. Ramsay gathered the Aubergine and L'Oranger staffs and told them of his plans. He offered anyone who wanted a job to come with him and work at his new place.

What happened next created quite a stir in the London restaurant scene, making headlines in the newspapers and throwing many diners into a mild panic. So many staff members walked out at that moment that both Aubergine and L'Oranger had to close.[3] Ramsay himself did not officially leave Aubergine for another four weeks, which was his required notice period.

A Place of His Own

Ramsay's ownership stake in Aubergine was small and, as it turned out, may not even have been real in the first place. He never actually saw his ownership shares. But all that did not seem to matter much once he was the sole owner of his own restaurant. There was plenty to do before the big opening. Many former staff members from Aubergine and L'Oranger who were loyal to Ramsay were willing to follow him to Royal Hospital Road. Consequently, staffing the new venture was relatively easy. His wife, Tana, helped decorate. Ramsay reportedly was determined to come up with a menu that would "wow" customers and make an even greater name for himself.

On September 1, 1998, Ramsay opened his new restaurant. In keeping with a trend followed by many famous chefs, Ramsay named his place after himself. The full name also took into account where the restaurant was located: Gordon Ramsay at Royal Hospital Road. Two solid months of hard work by Ramsay and his team had apparently paid off; the restaurant was a raging success. Ramsay has claimed that soon after opening Restaurant Gordon Ramsay, as the restaurant was also known, he was doing twice the business that La Tante Claire had done at that location. There was a long waiting list for reservations.

Ramsay's efforts to fine-tune the menu were well received. Moira Hodgson of the *London Observer* wrote:

> Mr. Ramsay's cooking is very good indeed. You get a sense of absolute confidence, of meticulous and unerring attention to detail. His dishes are so intense in flavor they seem rich, but in fact most of them are extraordinarily light.[4]

Ramsay met his wife, Tana, when she was dining at Aubergine. The couple married in London in 1996.

Hodgson also commended Ramsay for having earned two Michelin stars (while at Aubergine), and predicted he was "a serious contender for a third." As it turns out, she was correct about Ramsay receiving more stars. In fact, by 2001, Restaurant Gordon Ramsay held three Michelin stars—the highest rating possible. Ramsay had set himself a goal and met it.

"I felt vindicated," he said of the experience, "...like an actor who gets an Oscar or an NFL player who has a Super Bowl ring." Yet Ramsay knew he still faced a challenge. "And now that I've won them, how do I keep them?"[5] No problem on that score. Restaurant Gordon Ramsay has held on to all three stars, straight through the 2015 Michelin ratings.

Man With a Plan

Building off of Restaurant Gordon Ramsay's successful first year, Ramsay teamed up once again with Marcus Wareing to open Pétrus. Wareing was set to be the head chef at the new restaurant, which was located down the block from L'Oranger. The restaurant earned a Michelin star after being open for less than a year.

"I felt vindicated... like an actor who gets an Oscar or an NFL player who has a Super Bowl ring."

Pétrus marked the beginning of an expansion further into restaurant ownership by Ramsay. His business model was such that he would bring the Ramsay-inspired dining experience to various locations, first in London, then worldwide. Since he could not be in multiple places at the same time, he would act as owner and executive chef—kind of like a manager. The

Ramsay stands at the entrance to his successful restaurant, Gordon Ramsay at Royal Hospital Road (also known as Restaurant Gordon Ramsay). Opened in 1998, Ramsay's first solo venture earned the chef three Michelin stars in just a few years of operation.

day-to-day running of the restaurants and the bulk of the cooking would be done by head chefs hand-picked by Ramsay himself. Typically these chefs had worked with him for several years, so he knew he could trust them to run his restaurants on his behalf.

That does not mean that Ramsay planned to be a hands-off manager. Before every opening, he made it a point to be on site as often as possible. He offered guidance to his head chefs and tasted every dish that was to go on the menu a number of times until it met his satisfaction. Doing otherwise would have been impossible. "I'm too much of a control freak," Ramsay has said.[6]

Empire Builder

Several initial deals saw Ramsay take control of dining establishments within various hotels. These include the restaurant inside Claridge's, a five-star hotel in London's Mayfair district. Gordon Ramsay at Claridge's, as the restaurant was called, opened in 2001. Following soon after that same year was the opening of Amaryllis, housed in the hotel One Devonshire Gardens in Ramsay's native Glasgow, Scotland. Ramsay purchased and totally renovated the restaurant of another Mayfair hotel, The Connaught, which led to the opening of Gordon Ramsay at the Connaught in 2002.

In 2003, Ramsay took over operation of the world-famous Savoy Grill, situated in the historic Savoy Hotel. He put Wareing in charge of this restaurant as well as Pétrus, which had moved to a new location that same year. Once again a Ramsay-owned restaurant sprang up in the space formerly occupied by Pierre Hoffmann's La Tante Claire, in London's Berkeley Hotel. At about that time, negotiations for another chef to manage a second restaurant within the hotel had fallen through. Ramsay

★ First-Class Food

London's Heathrow Airport is one of the busiest in the world. Travelers barely have time to grab a snack before catching their flights. It is in this time-crunched environment that Ramsay set himself a new challenge—serving multiple-course gourmet meals in under half an hour.

Plane Food opened in Heathrow's Terminal 5 in 2008. The restaurant serves the same type of cuisine offered in Ramsay's other fine-dining establishments. Main dishes such as braised pork belly and saffron butter curry chicken are on the eat-in menu. There also are "cool boxes" with three courses packed and ready to take on a plane.

An estimated 20,000 fliers take advantage of Plane Food's offerings each month. Ramsay has said he would like to bring the Plane Food concept to several airports in the U.S. as well.[7] In the meantime he'll have to be content with the Heathrow location, as well as the consulting work he does for Singapore Airlines to provide fabulous in-flight meals.

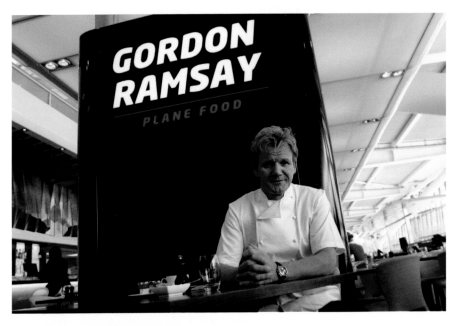

To the relief of travelers around the world, Ramsay opened Plane Food in Heathrow Airport in 2008. This fine dining restaurant also offers a limited take-out menu that allows passengers to enjoy a three-course meal in the air.

acquired that as well, later opening the Boxwood Café in its place. The Boxwood offered a more casual dining experience with traditional British dishes replacing French cuisine on the menu. There was even a children's menu, creating a family-friendly vibe.

Throughout the 2000s, Ramsay extended his culinary reach beyond the United Kingdom. Verre and Cerise repeated the tradition of running restaurants inside of hotels—the Dubai Hilton in the United Arab Emirates and Conrad Tokyo in Japan's capital city, respectively. Ramsay also owned or operated restaurants opened in Italy, France, South Africa, Australia and the Czech Republic. In the United States, he opened Gordon Ramsay at the London Hotel in New York City in 2006. Since then he has pushed his brand into the U.S. via Boca Raton, Florida; West Hollywood and Los Angeles, California; and Las Vegas, Nevada. While Ramsay later wound up closing several of his restaurants, beginning in 2009, he still has managed to keep a strong presence in Europe and the United States.

Chapter

4

Screen and
Page

After professional football, Ramsay had set his sights on becoming a world-class chef. And he had achieved that goal. Becoming a reality television star most likely never crossed his mind. Yet that is precisely what he has become, in the United Kingdom and the United States. Ramsay is undoubtedly as well known, if not more so, for his television appearances as he is for his cooking. There is a connection between these two worlds in which he lives. After all, his shows revolve around being a chef, running a restaurant, and other aspects of the hospitality business.

Another outlet for Ramsay's passion when it comes to food and cooking is the publication of cookbooks. In his 2006 autobiography, *Roasting in Hell's Kitchen*, Ramsay wrote that he has his own collection of about 3,500 cookbooks. By now, he probably has dozens, if not hundreds, more. The reason he owns so many is because he understands their value. Inexperienced cooks can get their feet wet following tested recipes found in cookbooks. Professionals such as Ramsay can be inspired by their contents. By writing cookbooks of his own, Ramsay is able to inspire others in their quest for cooking excellence.

Boiling Over the Top

Technically, Ramsay's first television appearance was as a judge for a reality culinary show in 1998, shortly after he had left Aubergine. However, British viewing audiences best remember his "starring" role in a 1998 British Broadcast Corporation (BBC) TV documentary titled *Boiling Point*.

The film, which aired in four segments, was meant to be a behind-the-scenes look at a popular restaurant and its up-and-coming chef. Unfortunately, it was filmed during a difficult time in Ramsay's career. He was getting Restaurant Gordon Ramsay up and running, under stress of his own making while trying to obtain a third Michelin star. Additionally, his former business partners at A-Z Restaurants were suing him. All that was combined with the hectic action that normally goes on in a fine-dining restaurant. The result was that Ramsay came off as a vulgar madman on camera. "I looked at a clip," Ramsay said of the show, years later, "and I saw that I needed controlling. I don't regret making it, because that was me at the time. But I was shocked. No one had ever shown me in real life."[1]

Still he also was proud of the telecast because it was so real and no-holds-barred. Tired of all the cooking shows on TV where things ran according to the script and the chefs were so polished, he believed the documentary succeeded at showing how a real restaurant kitchen operated. That included some hot tempers, shouting, and cursing.

Business was booming at Restaurant Gordon Ramsay after the show aired. People could not wait to get a reservation at the restaurant run by that crazy celebrity chef. So the show was a

> *"I looked at a clip and I saw that I needed controlling."*

Mr. Ramsay and
⭐ Chef Hyde

Ramsay has a reputation for being an angry man with a horrible temper. While he does not deny these claims, he points out that such is a hazard of his trade. "Every top chef in the world has a fiery temper and a passion that is second to none," he said in 2012. "I'm one of the very few that doesn't have an agenda when it comes to TV."[3]

Which begs another question: Does he play up his "fiery temper" for the television cameras? Several of his friends and crew believe that he must, because off-camera he is a decent, hard-working—although perfectionistic—man. His former boss Albert Roux thinks that television producers encourage Ramsay to be controversial, to increase ratings. "Gordon doesn't have a nasty bone in his body," said Roux. "That's not the real him."[4]

blessing and a curse, the latter because it made Ramsay look like a madman who was absolutely awful to his staff. Ramsay has long maintained that although his desire for perfection in the kitchen can make him a bit of a bully, the cursing maniac from *Boiling Point*—and its sequel, 2000's *Beyond Boiling Point*—was not the real him. "I don't want to sound like a sad [sack], because the film opened so many doors for me, but it was the wrong me."[2]

Fake It 'Til You Make It

In between the two *Boiling Point* telecasts, Ramsay was featured on an episode of the television reality series *Faking It*. In this show, ordinary people are chosen to perform a task they know little to nothing about well enough to fool a panel of judges. They are given four weeks to learn their new trade. Mentors who are professionals in the field contestants are entering, help along the way. Ramsay was one of two mentors to a burger-truck owner named Ed Devlin, who was supposed to become a master chef.

To say that Ramsay and Devlin got off to a rough start might be an understatement. Devlin would laugh while working, which angered Ramsay, who saw cooking as serious business. He showed Devlin how to handle a kitchen crew like a pro—by shouting at them constantly. The rookie's response to working in Ramsay's kitchen was classic: "I've never seen so many unhappy people. It's like hell." There were a few choice words for Chef Ramsay's management style as well. "I'm really glad I don't live in his head because it must be a really cold and sterile place. Like a curse."[5]

In the end, Devlin fooled the judges into thinking he was a professional chef. Ramsay was so pleased that he shouted, this time with joy, and hugged his pupil while the cameras were rolling. Television viewers and the British Academy of Film and Television Arts enjoyed the moment as well. The episode won a BAFTA Award for Best Factual Primetime Feature in 2001.

Nightmares in Hell

With his early appearances on the small screen, Ramsay had caught the attention of television executives in the United Kingdom. Soon he was in discussions with a production company to headline a show about trying to save failing restaurants. As with several of the restaurants he owned, the show would bear his name: *Ramsay's Kitchen Nightmares*. The program's original title was *Ramsay's Restaurant Rescues*. Allegedly he proclaimed that the kitchen of the first place where they were filming was "a nightmare," and the name stuck.[6]

The show premiered in England on April 27, 2004. The premise was that Chef Ramsay would spend a little more than a week working with the owners and staff of struggling restaurants. He would offer guidance and training, then come back in a month to see how the business is doing. Like during the taping of *Boiling Point*, Ramsay held nothing back. BBC censors were kept busy "bleeping" out some of the chef's most choice comments to his staff. If Ramsay's reputation as an angry, foulmouthed personality was not cemented after *Boiling Point* and its sequel, it certainly was after *Ramsay's Kitchen Nightmares* hit the airwaves.

Also in 2004, Ramsay hosted a show called *Hell's Kitchen*. In the British version of the show, celebrities competed against each other, serving meals they had prepared to other celebrity "customers." Viewers cast votes for their favorite chef. Ramsay was there to teach the celebrities to cook and offer commentary.

The success of *Ramsay's Kitchen Nightmares* led to a American version called *Kitchen Nightmares*. Both shows presented Ramsay with the task of reviving a failing restaurant.

He hosted the show only for the first of the four seasons it was broadcast in the U.K.

"F" Stands For "Food"

The success of his other shows led British television production company Optomen to offer Ramsay another show. *The F Word* was part information program, part cooking show, and part reality show. Correspondents reported on food matters from the field. During the first season, celebrities were taught how to cook dishes that were served to customers in a restaurant created specifically for the show. In later seasons, they either challenged Ramsay to a cook-off or chatted with the host while they dined. Commis chefs vied to work at a Ramsay restaurant, while amateur chefs competed to earn a chance to cook for a seating at either Claridge's or Ramsay at Royal Hospital Road. No matter the season, every episode revolved around one thing—food.

The F Word also featured segments where Ramsay traveled around the world on food-related adventures, often in search of unique and exotic ingredients. It was while filming one of these segments in Iceland that Ramsay received one of the biggest frights of his life. While hunting puffins, a type of bird, he slipped off a cliff and fell 280 feet into ice-cold water. Even though he was a good swimmer (thanks to his dad), he was wearing boots and heavy clothing, and he sank beneath the surface for quite a while.

"I was panicking and my lungs were filling with water," said Ramsay when recounting the event.[7] Thankfully the crew that was filming the hunt managed to throw him a rope and pull him back on dry land.

Ramsay's daughter Matilda has entered the family business. The teen hosts her own cooking show "Matilda and the Ramsay Bunch" for the CBBC network.

Limited Engagements

Over the years, Ramsay has popped up on televisions across the U.K. in shows that ran for a limited time, or a certain number of episodes. These specials have things in common with his multi-year series. For instance, much like *Hell's Kitchen, Ramsay's Best Restaurants* (nine episodes in 2010) is a reality show revolving around a competition. Teams from restaurants serving a variety of cuisines were pitted against each other for the title of "best restaurant" in England.

Gordon's Great Escape (three episodes in 2010, another four in 2011) borrowed the travel and adventure element from *The F Word*. The first series had Ramsay traveling to different parts of India in an attempt to learn more about the country's cuisine. In 2011 he visited four countries in South East Asia to learn how to prepare their native foods.

Gordon Ramsay's Ultimate Cookery Course (2012, twenty episodes) was a daytime, "how-to" cooking skills program. The show was broadcast around the same time that Ramsay's cookbook of the same name was published.

Gordon Ramsay Behind Bars, which aired in 2012, was something a bit different for the master chef. Instead of celebrities or hopeful commis, Ramsay was working with inmates in England's Brixton Prison. The idea was to teach the twelve men how to cook, in order to give them a skill they could use once they were released. The in-prison business they started, Bad Boys' Bakery, has sold packaged slices of lemon tart to area stores of the Caffé Nero coffee house chain. "This is reality TV with a conscience," wrote Decca Aitkenhead of the (London) *Guardian*, "more concerned with rehabilitation than fine dining."[8]

Celebrity Chef Jr.

It would seem as if having one's own cooking show runs in the Ramsay family. The chef's youngest daughter started taping *Matilda and the Ramsay Bunch* in 2014, for broadcast the following year. (Ramsay and his wife have four children: Megan, twins Jack and Holly, and Matilda.) The series is filmed in and around the family's home in Los Angeles. Each episode features Tilly, as she is called, making beginner-friendly recipes connected to family events and outings. She has made dishes that go with stunt lessons at a film studio, zip-lining, and surfing. Her dad frequently pesters her in the kitchen and tries to give her cooking tips. Tilly's typical response is to tell viewers, "He's so annoying."

The show came about when Ramsay's producers saw his daughter in action during filming in the family home. Ramsay says they saw something special in Matilda: "That level of confidence, the ability to have fun, hold your own, and call it like it is."[9]

Now Serving America

Ramsay has called bringing *Hell's Kitchen* to America "one of the more challenging experiences of my life."[10] By that he mostly meant getting used to the way things are done in the United States and being thrust into the glitz and glamour of the Hollywood lifestyle while taping in Los Angeles. Overall he was happy with the direction the show was taking. The U.K. version of the show had celebrities competing against each other. The American version featured real-life chef wannabes. Ramsay also was given creative control, especially when it came to culinary decisions. He admits that the money they were paying him, as well as the funds that the Fox Television Network pumped into the show itself, didn't hurt, either.

The American version of *Hell's Kitchen* first aired in 2005. Two years later, Ramsay began production of *Kitchen Nightmares* for Fox. The show was modeled on the U.K.'s *Ramsay's Kitchen Nightmares*. In 2012, Fox and Ramsay put a new spin on the "saving the business" format by debuting *Hotel Hell*. This show had Ramsay attempting to help the owners of troubled hotels, motels, and inns improve their businesses. The show was renewed, and was casting for its third season in 2015. Meanwhile, Ramsay had pulled the plug on *Ramsay's Kitchen Nightmares* in the U.K. and *Kitchen Nightmares* in the U.S. in the same year, 2014.

The idea for Ramsay's next show for Fox was based on the U.K. cooking-competition show *MasterChef*, on which Ramsay had appeared as a guest. Amateur chefs go up against each other through several rounds of competition to gain the title of master chef. The winner gets cash, a cookbook deal—and a trophy. But all of that combined comes in second to the real reason the amateurs compete, according to Ramsay. "This

Ramsay's television competition *Hell's Kitchen* has proved to be incredibly popular. Ramsay's colorful personality, particularly his legendary tantrums, is a significant reason.

Working with kids on *MasterChef Junior* allows Ramsay to show his lighter side. Rather than berating and screaming at the young contestants, Ramsay strives to inspire them.

search is all about the natural connection people have with food. They're not doing it for a job, they're doing it for a passion."[11]

In 2013, Ramsay and Fox launched a spinoff, *MasterChef Junior*. On this show, the contestants range in age from 8 to 13. While Ramsay could be demanding on the young chefs, he was hardly as tough on them as he was on adult contestants or commis in his restaurants. In fact, he has said it's difficult to watch the kids be hard on themselves when they make mistakes, or cry when they are eliminated. In the end, the show is not about crowning a winner. "I need to help them realize their potential," he said of *MasterChef Junior* contestants.[12]

Despite all his television exposure, Ramsay makes sure that he does not let the celebrity go to his head. He has said repeatedly that he puts his cooking first. "Being called a celebrity makes a mockery of how hard I have worked. ... Without the telly I am a serious chef, and on telly I am a serious chef."[13]

Passion for Cookbooks

Ramsay is the author of more than a dozen cookbooks. His first book, *Passion for Flavour*, won a Glenfiddich Award, recognizing excellence in food writing and broadcasting. Perhaps the work was award-winning because it was quite complex, maybe even a little bit fussy. The introduction even warned readers that the recipes were not for beginners.

By the time he was appearing on television in *Ramsay's Kitchen Nightmares*, however, he had a change or heart regarding his approach to writing. He began to see his TV shows and cookbooks as being linked tools in his mission to bring good food to the masses. Ramsay figured people would see him, or contestants, preparing food onscreen, then buy his books to get the recipes for those and other dishes. Also, the recipes were less

Once he had shared his love of cooking with restaurant customers and television viewers, Ramsay turned his attention to the home cook, authoring several cookbooks.

elaborate, although they still centered around fresh, healthful ingredients.

Ramsay has stressed that cookbooks—even his—cannot make someone a chef, or even a good cook. Recipes only go so far. Potential chefs also need to have a certain amount of natural talent. "It's all about flair and instinct," he said.[14]

Chapter

5

Beyond the
Kitchen

Gordon Ramsay trained for years to become a chef. Opening several restaurants and producing and/or starring in several television shows made him, by necessity, a businessman. For a celebrity chef, his name and his dishes have become what is known as a brand. The Gordon Ramsay brand is known worldwide. In order for the brand to keep its good reputation, the people behind it need to make smart business moves. Ramsay did not go to school to learn business. Instead, he surrounded himself with knowledgeable people, and learned as he went along—much as he did when he was becoming a chef.

Another point in Ramsay's favor on the business end of things is that he believed in his talent for food-related matters. Through the years he largely has trusted his instincts in that area and has gone in directions his gut tells him will be profitable.

Gordon Ramsay Holdings

In 1998, as he was preparing to open his first restaurant, Ramsay founded Gordon Ramsay Holdings (GRH), a holding company that would handle his business dealings. A holding company is a business that does not produce a product itself but essentially owns and manages other companies. It was under the GRH umbrella that Ramsay opened the bulk of his restaurants.

The cofounder of GRH was Chris Hutcheson, Ramsay's father-in-law. Early in his career, Ramsay had relied on Hutcheson to take the lead on complicated business matters while the chef worked more on the creative, cooking end. Which is not to say that Ramsay was not actively involved in corporate matters beyond the kitchen doors. He made sure to attend board meetings, even when he was working outside of London. Gillian Thomson, who was GRH director of operations in 2008, said that as a businessman, Ramsay was "always enthusiastically inspirational with an incredible eye for detail."[1]

Apparently he was no slouch on the restaurant end of the business either, even as his holdings and interests blossomed. "It doesn't matter how big we get," said GRH employee Mark Askew in 2008, "Gordon is always present to oversee menus and tastings, which brings a second level of security, appreciation, and an attention to detail to everything we do."[2]

In 2010, Ramsay and Hutcheson had a falling out, which resulted in the latter leaving the company. GRH then underwent some changes, including becoming a subsidiary, or lesser, company under a new parent company named Kavalake Limited. Under Ramsay's leadership, the company's restaurant holdings were made leaner and meaner. Several restaurants that were "underperforming," meaning not bringing in enough money to offset the cost of running them, were closed or entered into a licensing deal. Under the licensing agreements, Ramsay typically continued to provide menus and chefs. Licensed restaurants kept the Gordon Ramsay name, for which Ramsay

Chris Hutcheson (shown with wife Greta) is Ramsay's father-in-law and was responsible for Ramsay's business affairs until the two had a falling out.

received licensing fees, but Ramsay no longer owned them. Furthermore, Ramsay did not have to pay rent on the spaces used by the restaurants.[3]

After reorganizing company finances and re-evaluating his goals, Ramsay began to open new restaurants again. He has branched out in the Middle East to Qatar, to Hong Kong and Singapore in Asia, and to Atlantic City in the United States. Several other ventures have opened closer to home in the U.K.— including one in the space formerly occupied by Aubergine in Chelsea. Who says you can't go home again?

Potato Productions

With his restaurant empire covered by GRH, Ramsay decided to enter into a partnership with the U.K.'s Optomen Television to handle his television shows. His production company, One Potato Two Potato (OPTP), was formed in 2008. The company created and put shows on the air that made Ramsay a household name. Based in the U.K., One Potato Two Potato opened an office in the U.S., in Santa Monica, California, in early 2010. That office worked primarily on shows broadcast by the Fox Network, with whom Ramsay had a development deal. In other words, Ramsay and company were under contract to create new shows for Fox.

Later in 2010, All3Media, a giant production company based in England, bought One Potato Two Potato and Optomen. In exchange for his half-ownership of OPTP, Ramsay was paid a sum at the time of the sale plus more money over time, provided the company's shows met profit goals. All told, the deal was reported to be worth around 40 million pounds, or roughly $61.5 million.[4]

Ramsay believes in the importance of culinary education. As co-owner of Tante Marie, the chef gives lectures and offers apprenticeships at his restaurants to the very best students.

Home-Grown Talent

In 2009, England's oldest independent culinary school, Tante Marie, reopened its doors under new ownership. One of the co-owners was none other than Chef Gordon Ramsay. Tante Marie offers courses in cooking theory, but the majority of students' time is spent on more practical matters, actually cooking under the guidance of a teacher.

Guest lecturers, such as Ramsay himself, offer their wisdom in the classroom as well. A move to a larger location in 2014 allowed the school to operate an on-site restaurant, where students can serve an apprenticeship while working for their diploma. Also offered is "gap year" certificate course work—similar to the training Ramsay underwent as a young man. A gap yewar is traditionally a year off before commencing university studies. Young people often take the opportunity of a "free" year by traveling or by learning useful skills, such as the culinary arts.

"I'll bring back apprentice training on a national scale," said Ramsay when announcing his participation in the school, "and if anyone proves good enough at twenty-five they'll be running my kitchens."[5]

Under the terms of the agreement with All3Media, Ramsay would continue to star in and produce television shows in the U.K. and the U.S., including those produced for the Fox Network. Since 2010, OPTP also has been involved in producing shows for other networks. These include *My Kitchen*—a look at celebrity chefs' home lives and kitchens—for UKTV's Good Food Channel, and, in the United States, *Food Court Wars* for the Food Network and the Bravo network's reality competition show *Best New Restaurant*. The company also produces daughter Tilly's *Mathilda and the Ramsay Bunch*, broadcast on CBBC (the children's arm of the British Broadcasting Corporation, or BBC) in the U.K.

The Ramsay Seal of Approval

There is a lot of power behind the Ramsay name. Those who have signed licensing agreements that have kept his name on restaurants he has sold know it. All3Media proudly highlights Ramsay's connection to several of its shows produced by the chef or through OPTP. The association between the name Gordon Ramsay and excellence is the main reason why so many companies have hired the celebrity chef to help sell their products.

Ramsay has endorsement deals for many products in the U.K. Among the companies he has promoted are gourmet-flavored Walkers Crisps (potato chips), Gordon's Gin, British optical retail chain Specsavers, and telecommunications firm BT. Australia saw him reduced to doing dishes and taking out the trash, because Perfect Italiano cheeses made cooking so easy, his chef services weren't needed. He also has appeared in commercials for Acura, Capitol One, and AT&T that have aired in the U.S.

As if his restaurant and television empire were not enough, Ramsay has endorsed a number of products in the US and UK. Staying in the public eye has made him a household name.

Ramsay has teamed up with presitgious tableware manufacturer Royal Doulton to produce a popular line of cookware, knives, place settings, and serving pieces.

Beyond simply being a pitchman for other companies, Ramsay has also cut deals to sell cooking and dining products that bear his name and/or likeness. Fine-china manufacturer Royal Doulton sells a line of Gordon Ramsay tableware and cookware. In spots promoting the dishes, knives, casseroles, pots, and pans, Ramsay tells viewers that items used in his restaurants inspire the designs for these items. Royal Doulton currently sells lines by Ramsay named after his Maze and Bread Street restaurants. A line of small appliances also is sold by a separate manufacturer under the brand name Gordon Ramsay Everyday.

Business Lessons Learned

In his autobiography, Ramsay recalled a time when the head chef at Hotel Diva tried to make him take the blame for a huge mistake in the kitchen on an important night at the restaurant. Even though he was only a commis, he refused the head chef's demand. It wasn't so much that he was afraid of getting in trouble. It was more a matter of principle.

"Lying is the biggest sin you can commit in a kitchen," Ramsay wrote. "Working with someone who lies to you is worse than working with someone who can't cook."[6]

With that, Ramsay had defined one of the bigger lessons he has learned when it comes to business: know

> *"Lying is the biggest sin you can commit in a kitchen. Working with someone who lies to you is worse than working with someone who can't cook."*

77

Although he is incredibly busy, Ramsay manages to find time to spend with his family. This 2002 snapshot shows Gordon and Tana with (left to right) Megan, Jack, and Holly Ramsay.

whom to trust. That is why the chefs he has hired to run his restaurants in his absence have worked with him and for him over several years. After his dealings with A-Z Restaurants and issues with business partner (and father-in-law) Chris Hutcheson, Ramsay also learned never to take anything at face value alone. Had he paid even a little more attention to the account books, or questioned his partners in both cases more thoroughly, a lot of trouble could have been avoided.

Arguably, Ramsay also learned that it is not good to expand too rapidly. He was riding a strong wave of success and public approval when he opened restaurants at a blazing pace during the early 2000s. He also parlayed his television celebrity into multi-show deals on both sides of the Atlantic Ocean. While it is important to strike while the iron is hot, it is also wise to know one's limits and not get overextended, in terms of both time and money.

One lesson learned in the world of business that Ramsay seems to have known all along is to love what you do and put your all into making it a success. "I go into every restaurant, every program, as if it's the first day," he has said. "And I give 110 percent. Because it's not that money that turns me on. I find that side slightly embarrassing. It's wonderful and it's nice, but it doesn't make you a better chef. The fundamental crux of a successful chef is being true to what you do."[7]

Chapter
6

Awards and
Honors

Gordon Ramsay has made it clear, time and again, that the award that matters most to him as a chef comes in the form of a Michelin star, and the more the merrier. This is a tough man who publicly admitted to being quite upset when his Gordon Ramsay at the London Hotel restaurant in New York City—the first restaurant he opened in the United States—lost two of its three stars in one fell swoop. "I started crying when I lost my stars," he told a Norwegian talk show host in 2014. "It's a very emotional thing for any chef. It's like losing a girlfriend. You want her back."[1]

Yet no matter how prestigious they are, the Michelin rankings are not the only game in town when it comes to honoring the world's top chefs. Other organizations offer their own awards and acknowledgements. Perhaps not surprisingly, Ramsay has been the recipient of several of those in addition to his lifetime (thus far) total of 14 stars.

A Nod or Two From Harden's

In the early 1990s, brothers Richard and Peter Harden created a guidebook, the likes of which their fellow Londoners had never seen before. The first *Harden's London Restaurants* was designed after guides in other European cities where the brothers were working at the time. While Michelin stars are awarded based on reviews written by professional "inspectors," *Harden's* guides rely on general-public surveys to decide their rankings. Restaurants are rated on a five-star system that measures food, service, and ambiance, or atmosphere.

Ramsay and his restaurants have been awarded a number of *Harden's* stars over the years. In fact,

> **"I started crying when I lost my stars. It's a very emotional thing for any chef."**

the guidebooks voted him London's Best Chef eleven years in a row, beginning in 1995. His first restaurant, Gordon Ramsay at Royal Hospital Road, was listed as one of the city's top restaurants for twelve years running, beginning in 2001. Survey respondents chose five of Ramsay's fine-dining establishments as their top ten best meals.[2]

Harden's is not the only culinary authority to recognize Ramsay's status among the U.K.'s best chefs. In 2006, *The Caterer* magazine called him "the most influential and high-profile chef-restaurateur to emerge in recent years."[3] Prior to that, Ramsay received what must have been an even greater honor, because it came from his peers. In a 2003 *Caterer* survey of Michelin star-holding chefs, Ramsay was voted the U.K.'s third-greatest living chef, after his mentors the Albert and Michel Roux, and Marco Pierre White.[4]

Gordon Ramsay has received much acclaim during his career as a chef, including winning Restaurant of the Year at the 2003 Tio Pepe Carlton London Restaurant Awards.

The Cateys

Every industry should have a glamorous gala event, where excellence in the field is applauded and rewarded. In the U.K. culinary scene, that event is the annual Caterer and Hotelkeeper Awards, nicknamed the Cateys. The awards are sponsored by *The Caterer* magazine.

The awards ceremony has been called British hospitality's version of the Oscars. Nominations come from U.K. hospitality workers, who also vote to see who wins the award in each of twenty-two categories. Once ballots have been cast and counted, hospitality workers from across the United Kingdom gather for a black-tie dinner, followed by the presentation of the awards.

Ramsay is only the third person to have racked up three Catey wins in their careers. His first win, for Newcomer of the Year, came in 1995, when he was head chef at Aubergine. In 2000, he captured the highly desirable Chef of the Year Award. His third Catey was for Independent Restaurateur of the Year, awarded in 2006.

Even bigger than a Catey was an honor bestowed upon Ramsay in 2006. That's when Queen Elizabeth appointed Ramsay an Officer of the Order of the British Empire. Ramsay received this honor for having a major local and national role in the hospitality industry.

Awards for "Telly"

Ramsay also has been recognized for his work on television. As mentioned earlier, his episode on the series *Faking It* won an award from the British Academy of Film and Television Arts, or BAFTA. In addition to its annual major awards ceremony, the Academy stages a number of events that support the television,

Perhaps one of Ramsay's greatest honors was being named Officer of the Most Excellent Order of the British Empire (OBE) for his contributions to the hospitality industry.

Gordon the
★ Emmy-less

Hard as it may be to believe, since he is such a fixture on television, Ramsay has never won an Emmy Award. The Emmys honor excellence in prime time television programming in the United States. Granted, Ramsay has a couple of BAFTA awards, which is the U.K. equivalent to the Emmy. Still, this gaping hole in his trophy case has not gone unnoticed, or un-commented-upon, by Ramsay.

"The Emmys to me would be like a Michelin star," he told a reporter in 2012 when asked what winning an Emmy would mean to him. "It's the Oscars of the TV world. For me it's the shining jewel in the crown I haven't got yet."[5]

film, and gaming arts. Ramsay was also nominated for a BAFTA in 2005, for his work on *Kitchen Nightmares*, and a 2008 Scottish BAFTA award for Most Popular Scottish Presenter.

The Australian Subscription Television and Radio Association (ASTRA) honored Ramsay two years in a row. In 2008 and 2009, he was nominated for, and won, the Astra Award for Favourite International Personality or Actor. The award stemmed from his work on the U.S. version of *Hell's Kitchen*.

Among the other award nominations Ramsay has received are the U.K. National Television Awards (Most Popular TV Expert, 2005), the People's Choice Awards (Favorite TV Chef, 2011), the Critics Choice Television Awards (Best Reality Host, 2013 and 2014), and the Online Film & Television Association Awards (Best Host or Panelist in a Non-Fiction Program, 2014).

Going the Distance

Under a great deal of stress when he opened his first restaurant in 1998, Ramsay did what a lot of people do in such a situation—he ate. When he got to be around 270 pounds, he knew it was time to act. In addition to watching what he ate, he hit the road and took up running. Of course, simply running would not be enough for someone as driven and competitive as Ramsay. He chose to train for and compete in the London Marathon.

Since then, Ramsay has run in numerous endurance races, meaning marathons and ultra, or double, marathons. He also has participated in triathlons—which feature swimming and biking along with running—and even a few Iron Man competitions, which are an extreme form of triathlon.

As a chef and foodie, Ramsay understands the importance of properly fueling one's body before a big race. Four days before a competition, he works to rid his body of "toxic" substances

Ramsay was awarded a Scottish
BAFTA for his episode of the 2001
television series Faking It, in
which he transformed a burger
flipper into a fine dining chef.

A stress eater who spends his days and nights surrounded by food, Ramsay began competing in marathons, triathlons, Iron Man races, and other endurance competitions in 1998.

(for an athlete, at least), such as fats and cream. He powers up by eating plenty of pasta—risotto, specifically—vegetables, and fish. During the race, he takes every opportunity to rehydrate by sipping water at every station along the course.[6]

Charity Involvement

In his spare time—what little there may be—Ramsay devotes his time and energy to a handful of worthy causes. He is tremendously involved in the Scottish Spina Bifida Association, hosting, and cooking for, an annual luncheon through his "F is for Fundraising" appeal.[7] Ramsay has pledged to raise £450,000 each year to help fund support services for a spina bifida center he helped open.[8]

Ramsay has even found a way to incorporate his past and current careers into his charity work. His past as a footballer proved useful when, in 2006, when he played in a charity match titled England vs. the Rest of the World. This biennial event (every two years) has raised millions for UNICEF. Unfortunately, Ramsay, who captained the Rest of the World squad, played limited minutes due to an injury he received in training.

In 2007, Ramsay used his culinary skills to launch a line of condiments called Seriously Good sauces. A portion of every sale went to charity. Between 2007 and 2012, when the product was no longer available on store shelves, Seriously Good sauces raised £470,000 for Comic Relief, a U.K. charity that fights poverty worldwide.

More recently, Ramsay and his wife launched The Gordon Ramsay Foundation. In an attempt to make good on his pledge to raise more than $3 million by 2016, the foundation sponsored a fitness club where people could train to complete in a half-Iron Man event in 2015. Anyone wishing to take part in the

His charity endeavors have Ramsay lending time and money to many worthy causes. One is supporting The Rising Foundation, which is dedicated to helping at-risk youth in New Zealand.

club was required to pay a fee in excess of $4,000 and agree to raise the same amount in charitable pledges. All monies went to charities such as Cancer Research UK, Action Against Hunger, and the Scottish Spina Bifida Association.

No Time to Slow Down

Provided they do not get tired of the business or lose their inspiration, celebrity chefs can have a pretty long shelf life, meaning the length of time during which they are able to work. However, restaurant life can take a toll on a person's health, given the stress and possibility of kitchen accidents, let alone the fact that chefs work through their entire shifts with few if any breaks. Even the best may entertain the idea of calling it quits. Not surprisingly, coming from a man who has said on numerous occasions that he lives to work, Ramsay's told a reporter that his idea of retirement involves opening another restaurant.

"I'm gonna buy a boat, go down to the Virgin Islands and buy a restaurant," he said. "... Close it six days a week and open it one day a week. Just one day a week. I'll fish and dive the other days."[9]

Given his drive, work ethic, and passion for food, Ramsay should be around a good long time.

Chapter 7

Following in Gordon's
Footsteps

Gordon Ramsay did not begin to think seriously about a career as a chef until he was out of high school. His daughter Matilda already knew she liked cooking—and had her own television cooking show—by the age of thirteen, a good six years younger than her father. The younger one starts working toward their goal of working in a professional kitchen, the better. Training and taking classes as soon as possible can give potential chefs a definite advantage toward reaching their career goals.

Students can take the route Gordon Ramsay did, which is to enroll in professional classes through a college or trade school. Some might skip, or hold off on, that step and get right to work in the food-service industry. Either way, nobody starts off as a master chef. Everyone has to pay his or her dues, working one's way up the career ladder. The most obvious way for future chefs to learn their trade is by cooking as often as they can, professionally, as a hobby, or simply making family meals in their own homes. Examining how Ramsay built his career as a celebrated chef can give culinary wannabes plenty of important information about their own futures. Let's take a closer look at what it means to be a chef, and what it takes to get there, using Ramsay occasionally as an example.

Part of the Brigade

A good place to start is by defining the type of chefs one can become. Gordon Ramsay wanted to work in a first-class, fine-dining establishment, eventually becoming the executive chef of his own restaurant or—even better— restaurants. In a restaurant environment, the kitchen runs under a system known as a brigade.[1] "Brigade" typically is used as a military term, referring to a group of soldiers working together while following orders. The word is appropriate when applied to a professional kitchen because that is how a successful restaurant is supposed to be run—with military correctness and orderliness.

Chefs start out in the brigade a commis, which is basically a chef-in-training. Ramsay started as a commis several times, each time he landed a new job in a restaurant. These chefs do a little bit of everything, learning to work at each of several stations found in a professional kitchen.

Kitchen stations typically cover different types of food, including meat, vegetable, fish, and pastry. There is even a station dedicated to the creation of sauces and sautéed dishes, called the saucier station. The next step up from commis is to become a station chef. Ramsay worked his way up to manning the fish station when he worked at Guy Savoy in Paris.

With a lot of hard work and dedication, a chef who has experience running one or more stations may be tapped to become a sous chef. Considered the second-in-command, a sous chef is basically an assistant manager of the kitchen. Ramsay

Professional kitchens are commonly divided into distinct stations, with each chef working exclusively on the items for which his or her station is responsible, such as meat, seafood, salads, or sauces.

was sous chef of the kitchen at Harvey's for a time, under Marco Pierre White.

The role of manager in a restaurant kitchen belongs to the head chef, also referred to as the executive chef. Ramsay was the head chef at Aubergine before striking out on his own with Restaurant Gordon Ramsay.

Executive Chef Job Description

First and foremost, all types of chefs cook. But there are other job duties assigned to the different types of chefs or cooks, whether they are in a kitchen brigade or elsewhere. Starting at the top, executive chefs are in charge of everything that goes on in the kitchen. With regard to the food, they cover many tasks, from preparation and actual cooking to plating meals, meaning how the food is presented and looks on the plate.

As Ramsay did when he opened Gordon Ramsay at Royal Hospital Road, executive chefs create dishes and write menus. Then they teach the chefs under them how to prepare dishes according to their recipes.

In order to cook, chefs must have access to ingredients. Executive chefs oversee the ordering of the food with which the staff creates meals. They must make sure that supplies are always on hand, and that all purchases stay within budget. Making sure that ingredients are fresh and the best quality possible also falls to the executive chef.

Executive chefs have a lot more on their work plates than food. The responsibility for what everyone else in the kitchen does and how they act falls to them. Many executive chefs are so busy with the administrative, or managerial, tasks associated with the job that they leave most of the actual cooking to their "under chefs."

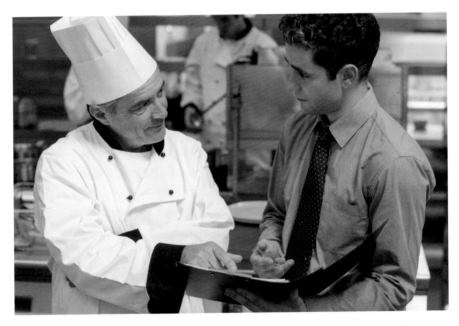

Head chefs are responsible for all of the operations in a restaurant kitchen, including managing staff, working with front-of-house management, and ordering supplies.

In With
★the Assist

As assistant chefs, sous chefs take on some managerial tasks in order to assist the head chef. They make sure that the orders and requirements handed down by the head chef are followed. They also report back to the executive chef on each night's performance in the kitchen, and attempt to resolve issues with customers. Sous chefs supervise the kitchen staff from a front-line position, resolving disagreements and making sure no one falls behind on the job. Often they also are in charge of scheduling workdays and shifts. And of course, sous chefs cook, taking a lead role in this regard when the head chef is away.

Because they are usually a one-person crew, personal chefs perform many of the same tasks as executive chefs do. The one exception is that they do not supervise staff.

Paths to Learning the Trade

The two best ways to learn how to become a chef are to take classes and to practice cooking, preferably while working with respected and successful chefs. Ramsay did both these things early on in his career. That move worked out very well for him, and it could for others as well. As Ramsay has said, "If you want to become a great chef, you have to work with great chefs."[2]

> *"If you want to become a great chef, you have to work with great chefs."*

Training can start as early as grade school or high school. The majority of school districts in the United States offer Family and Consumer Science classes. Formerly called Home Economics, these classes teach students the fundamentals of running a household, which includes budgeting and shopping for food, storing and cooking it safely, and serving it in an appealing way. Several community education programs and cooking schools also offer one-time or multi-week cooking classes for children and teenagers.

Anyone who is serious about cooking for a living should consider signing up for post-secondary (after high school) culinary courses after graduation. Many community colleges and four-year universities offer hospitality programs; culinary arts are part of this field. Courses in hotel management and other travel- and tourism-related subjects are generally required to receive a college or university associate or bachelor's degree in

One step to take on your path to becoming a chef is to take classes that offer cooking instruction. Your school might offer a class in Family and Consumer Sciences (FCS), also known as home economics.

Certifiably ★ Culinary

In many ways, getting certified as a chef is as useful as receiving a full-fledged degree. A certificate shows employers that its holder is knowledgeable in the field and can be trusted to do a good job. In order to be certified, candidates must meet certain requirements. These include level of education and continuing education credits earned. Some certification programs only require a high school or G.E.D. diploma, plus a set number of hours attending food-related classes or events. A candidate's level of on-the-job experience and passing a written exam generally are the other requirements for certification.

Being certified as a chef is not a necessity for landing a good job. However, many professionals in the culinary field highly recommend achieving, and keeping, certification. It should be considered an extra advantage in the competitive kitchen workplace.

hospitality. Students can typically complete a major—meaning a heavy emphasis on certain types of classes—in food and beverage or the culinary arts, but cooking will not be the only thing studied. One advantage of choosing this path is that students learn a lot about the business end of running a restaurant, which is something an executive chef needs to know.

For those who would rather have more hands-on time cooking in the kitchen, enrolling in a culinary arts school may be the way to go. Course work at one of these types of schools revolves completely around food, cooking, and running a food-service business. It is worth noting that students hoping to become pastry chefs can participate in special training that focuses on baking, instead of the more general preparation and cooking that would be necessary for other aspiring chefs.

Most culinary arts schools offer associate and bachelor's degrees after completion of study, much like community colleges and four-year universities. Certification programs are usually available as well. Many culinary arts schools require students to have either some formal cooking training, in high school or college, or anywhere from six months to a year of experience in a sit-down restaurant. Cooking burgers at the grill of a fast-food restaurant chain does not count.

Culinary schools typically have an internship or apprenticeship program attached to them. Interns and apprentices learn by working in the food service industry while they are still students enrolled in school. Students receive class credit toward their degrees while receiving first-hand experience in their chosen field.

Attending a culinary school will teach you all the basic methods, techniques, and skills needed by a chef starting out. In addition, the school can connect you with internships and apprenticeships where you can continue your learning.

Skillfully Done

Whether they are learned in a classroom or on the job, there are a number of skills that aspiring chefs must master to earn and keep a position in a kitchen. The basics include knife skills, cooking methods, and what's known in the trade as *mis en place*. *Mis en place* is a French cooking term that refers to having everything organized and in its proper place.

Chefs in training usually have what is known as a knife wallet. This wallet, or carrying case, contains several types of knives. The number and type of knives depend on the chef's skill level and preference. A chef's knife, which is actually what the tool is called, is a large-bladed chopping knife. It is one of the most-used knives in a professional chef's kitchen. A fillet knife has a long, thin blade that is used for cutting loose the flesh of fish. Boning knives are used to separate less delicate meat than fish from bone. The paring or utility knife has a small blade and is mainly used to peel and cut up fruit and vegetables. There are different kinds of cutting methods a chef must know and use, no matter the type of knife. These include slicing, mincing, and dicing.

Cooking methods are divided into two main categories: dry-heat cooking and moist-heat cooking. Dry-heat methods include baking or roasting, broiling, grilling, pan fry, and sauté. Blanching, boiling, poaching, simmering, and steaming are among the moist-heat methods a chef uses to get dishes cooked.

In a professional kitchen, the pace is fast and furious. Chefs can't waste time looking for items they need or preparing ingredients. Instead, each station has items prepared and ready to go, according to what dishes are on the menu, including specials. The vegetables are washed, peeled (if necessary), and cut up into the correct sized pieces, and are then placed in bulk containers. Meat is also cut in a way that serves the recipe, with bones and skin removed, and placed where handy in the refrigerator. Seasonings and spices are clearly labeled and easy to reach.

This concept of *mis en place* extends well beyond ingredients, or even pots, pans, and cooking utensils such as spoons, ladles, and spatulas. Professional chefs must be ready for anything. Also, they have to constantly keep in mind how to prepare all the items that go on a plate so that diners at each table receive their meals at the same time.

Where the Jobs Are

When people think of being a chef, they usually imagine someone working in the kitchen of a busy restaurant. However, some chefs work in other types of locations. Essentially any location that has a working kitchen could hire a chef or cook. Nursing homes, hospitals, schools, convention centers, and more hire people with a culinary background or industrial (large-group) cooking experience. Still others work as personal chefs for individuals in their employers' homes, or as caterers who cook for special events.

Chefs who are just starting out in the business can find open positions in a couple of different ways. Those who work as an apprentice already have their foot in the door. Sometimes students do so well that they are hired by the restaurant or organization where they served their apprenticeship. Checking out career websites is another way to find out who is hiring. There are several websites, such as Caterer.com, which are designed specifically for job seekers in the hospitality industry. Another way to obtain a chef's job is to gain a position—any position— in the kitchen or dining area of a fine restaurant. Working one's

Gordon Ramsay chose to begin his training in an academic setting before working in restaurant kitchens. However, there are several different paths a chef may take.

way up can happen no matter what a person's job title may initially be. After all, Ramsay started out washing dishes, and even did a little table service, before he found his way into the kitchen as a commis.

Near or Far, Working Hard

Ramsay also made a point of traveling from his home in Scotland to the city of London, then abroad to Paris, to learn his craft. Anyone who has the time and money to follow exactly in his footsteps could have the career adventure of a lifetime. Perhaps these folks might even land a job with one of the restaurants overseen by the former Gordon Ramsay Holdings. Many chefs like to spend time in kitchens in France to learn classic French techniques or in other restaurants abroad so they can broaden their cooking knowledge. However, moving around or even away from one's home is not necessary. People can become chefs no matter where they are.

That does not mean that aspiring chefs should settle for less than the best, though. Getting a job in a place that has a reputation for good food and service is a smart move. Young chefs who are just starting out should read culinary magazines and restaurant reviews, visit websites, and listen to word of mouth to find out where the hot spots and hot chefs are in their area. They should also trust their own taste buds, deciding where they think the food is the best by tasting it for themselves. Above all, the great chefs are interested in food, and they travel the globe to taste the offerings at fine restaurants and street vendors. The next step is to approach the management of the best establishments around and ask if they are hiring.

Those who work very hard should wind up making themselves indispensable, meaning absolutely necessary. That is what Ramsay did when he was starting out, and he ended up running the show at Windham Arms, as well as becoming Marco Pierre White's second-in-command. Any chef should quickly rise through the ranks of the kitchen brigade by having a passion for cooking, and letting that passion shine through in his or her work. In this way, they can carve out a successful and satisfying career as a chef.

Try It Yourself!

Stuffed Zucchini Rolls

Serves 4-8

Ingredients:

4 small zucchini, ends trimmed

Cherry tomatoes

1 glove of garlic, minced

3-4 tbsp. olive oil, plus extra to drizzle

3-4 tbsp. balsamic vinegar, to drizzle

8 oz. (230 g) ricotta

Juice of ½ a lemon

Zest of one lemon

Handful fresh basil leaves, chopped

½ cup (45 g) Parmesan cheese

Salt and pepper, to taste

Directions

1.) Slice the zucchini in long, thin strips. Lay the strips flat on a baking sheet, trying not to let them overlap.

2.) Drizzle with olive oil and balsamic vinegar and sprinkle with salt and pepper. Leave these to marinate in the fridge for about twenty-thirty minutes.

3.) In a medium-sized bowl combine ricotta, some of the basil, and salt and pepper to taste. Stir well until combined evenly.

4.) In another bowl, combine cherry tomatoes, basil, lemon zest, 2 tbsp. olive oil and 1 teaspoon of balsamic vinegar. Stir until combined.

5.) On a baking sheet, lay all tomatoes evenly, and cook in the oven until flattened and roasted, about ten minutes.

6.) Place 1 teaspoon of the ricotta mixture onto one end of a zucchini strip and gently roll up until a pinwheel forms. Repeat until you have used up all of the filling.

7.) Preheat oven to 350°F (175°C).

8.) Lay the rolls flat in an oven-safe casserole dish and bake for about 10-15 minutes, or until zucchini is tender.

9.) Once the tomatoes are cool enough to handle, place a tomato on top of each roll and hold in place with a toothpick. Arrange on a plate to serve as an appetizer, or place on plates to make it a main dish.

Croque Monsieur

Serves 4

Ingredients

8 slices sourdough bread

2 tbsp. (30 g) butter

1 tbsp (15 mL) all-purpose flour

1 ½ cups (12 oz./350 mL) milk

Sprinkle of freshly grated nutmeg (or ground)

Dijon (spicy) mustard

1 ¼ cups (280g) grated cheese (a mixture of
   Emmental (or Swiss), Gruyere (or Gouda)
   and sharp Cheddar is good)

1/3 lb. (150g) sliced ham, preferably smoked

Salt and pepper, to taste

Directions

For Béchamel:

1.) In small saucepan, melt 1 tbsp. butter.

2.) Stir in 1 tbsp. flour until a thick roux forms. You'll know when this happens because the butter will have browned the flour slightly, and the mixture will resemble a paste.

3.) Slowly whisk in the milk, being sure to scrape the edges of the pan. Use a light circular movement with your wrist, and continually beat the sauce. This will prevent lumps from forming and hurting your hand. Bring the sauce to a boil.

4.) Add salt, pepper, and sprinkle of nutmeg.

5.) Cook for an additional two-three minutes, or until it is thick and creamy.

6.) Remove from heat immediately.

For the sandwich:

1.) Lightly toast sourdough on each side, and then butter one side of each slice.

2.) Preheat Oven to 350°F (175°C).

3.) Spread a bit of the Dijon mustard on the buttered side of one of the pieces of toast, and some béchamel on top of that. Then, cover with grated cheese and a couple of slices of ham.

4.) Spread some béchamel on a slice of dry toast, and cover the ham and cheese. This will help the sandwich to stay together.

5.) Cover with béchamel and a bit more cheese.

6.) Repeat with remaining ingredients and bake for about eight minutes, or until crisp around the edges.

7.) Serve immediately. You can use any remaining béchamel as a dipping sauce, if desired.

Ratatouille

Serves 4

Ingredients:

1 large red onion, peeled

2 carrots, sliced

2 stalks of celery, chopped

1 small eggplant, diced

1 red and 1 yellow bell pepper, halved, cored, seeded and diced

1 large zucchini or yellow squash, diced

Juice of one lemon

5 tbsp. (75mL) olive oil

Sea salt and black pepper

2 large cloves of garlic, minced

1 (14 oz. can) chopped tomatoes, drained

8 oz. (230 g) fresh cherry tomatoes, sliced

A small handful of basil leaves, roughly torn

A few thyme sprigs

One large sprig of rosemary

A few sprigs of oregano

Directions

1.) In a large pan, pour 3 tbsp. olive oil, some salt, and the carrots, sautéing for about three minutes over high heat, or until the carrots begin to brown and soften.

2.) Turn heat down to medium-high.

3.) Add onion, and celery, and cook until they start to sweat and smell delicious. (Celery, onions, and carrots are what is called in the French culinary arts, a mirepoix). Add garlic, the rest of the olive oil, and pepper to taste.

4.) Turn the heat down to medium and add the eggplant, zucchini, peppers, and tomatoes, sautéing for about four minutes, or until the squash begins to soften.

5.) Using a piece of non-colored twine or string, tie the sprigs of herbs together (except for the basil). Drop those in the pan along with the lemon juice. When a few bubbles start to form, turn down the temperature to low or simmer.

6.) Cover the dish and cook for about eight-ten minutes more, or until the vegetables are all tender.

7.) Toss with basil before serving with crusty French bread and butter.

Farfalle with Peas and Bacon

Serves 4

Ingredients

14 ounces (400g) farfalle (bow-tie) pasta

1 tbsp. (15mL) olive oil

1 tbsp. (15mL) butter

8 slices bacon, chopped

1 garlic clove, finely chopped

1 cup (240mL) heavy cream

6 oz. (170g) peas, thawed if frozen

3 oz. (90g) Parmesan or Romano cheese, freshly grated, plus extra to sprinkle

1 small handful sage leaves

Parsley leaves, finely chopped

Directions

1.) Bring a pot of water to a boil. Add a generous sprinkle of coarse sea salt and add farfalle to the water. Cook according to package instructions (about seven-eight minutes for *al dente*).

2.) In a separate pan, melt the butter and olive oil and add bacon pieces, cooking over high heat for three-four minutes or until the bacon is brown. Be sure to step back to avoid any splatter.

3.) Add garlic and fry for a minute or two, or until the garlic is fragrant.

4.) Slowly pour in the cream, stirring gently with a rubber spatula or wooden spoon so that all the bacon drippings and garlic get fully incorporated into the cream. Bring to a gentle boil, and then turn down heat to low. Allow to simmer for about five minutes, or until sauce has thickened slightly (it will lessen in amount, or "reduce". This is exactly how it's supposed to be).

5.) Stir in the peas slowly, standing back to avoid any splashes. Cook for another three minutes or so.

6.) Meanwhile, pull the sage leaves from the stem, and clap them between the palms of your hands. This releases the oils and makes the sage more pungent.

7.) Add sage and some fresh pepper to sauce, along with grated cheese.

8.) Carefully drain the farfalle pasta and add it to the sauce, stirring until pasta is coated.

9.) Garnish with parsley and more cheese if desired.

Chicken with Creamy Thyme Dijon Sauce

Serves 4

Ingredients:

4 large chicken breasts or thighs

Sea salt and freshly ground black pepper

3-4 tbsp. (45-60mL) olive oil

1 tbsp. (15 g) butter

3 cloves of garlic, chopped

1 tbsp. (15 mL) of Dijon mustard

A few sprigs of fresh thyme, leaves removed from the stems

½ cup (120mL) heavy cream

Sprinkle of flour

Directions

1.) In a large skillet, place oil over medium-high heat.

2.) Season chicken with salt and pepper and place in skillet carefully.

3.) Brown chicken on both sides, about four-five minutes on each side.

4.) Cover and let cook for an additional fifteen minutes, or until the chicken juices are clear.

5.) Remove the chicken from the pan.

6.) Remove the thyme leaves from the stem by holding the top of the sprig with your fingertips and slowly pulling down the wood with your other fingers, against the leaf growth. You will collect the leaves in your hand.

7.) Melt butter in the pan, scraping the sides with a rubber spatula or a wooden spoon, in order to collect the bits of flavor left over from the chicken cooking.

8.) Slowly stir in the cream.

9.) Add thyme leaves, Dijon mustard, and sprinkle of flour. Stir vigorously for about six minutes, or until the sauce has thickened. Remove from heat.

10.) Pour over sauce over chicken and serve with vegetables and/or rice.

Fish and Chips

Serves 4

500g (18oz) white fish
fillets (such as pollock,
cod, haddock, or orange
roughy), skinned

1 tsp. dried dill

1 tsp. paprika

1 tsp. garlic or onion
powder

100g (3½ oz) panko
breadcrumbs

4 tbsp. plain flour

2 medium eggs, beaten

½ cup half and half or
whole milk

Oil, for frying (enough to cover the bottom of
the pan for up to 1 ½ inches), sunflower,
canola, or vegetable, or some combination
of the three

Sea salt and freshly ground black pepper

Malted vinegar or lemon juice for dipping

Directions

1.) Slice the filets into chunks (two or three per filet).
Place in the fridge to firm up while you prepare your
batter (the batter sticks better if the fish is cold when
it's battered).

2.) In a bowl, combine breadcrumbs, flour, and seasonings.

3.) In another bowl, beat the two eggs.

4.) Add milk to eggs, stirring until a creamy butter yellow mixture forms. This is called an egg wash.

5.) Pour oil into large skillet, enough to cover the bottom of the pan in one-two inches of oil. Turn heat to high, making sure the room is well ventilated.

6.) As the oil heats, dip a piece of fish into the egg wash, making sure that it is fully coated. Shake off any extra.

7.) After the filet is coated in egg wash, dip it into the breadcrumb/flour/seasoning mixture. Pat the breading into the fish, making sure that each surface it totally covered in breading. Repeat with all the pieces of fish.

8.) Test the oil's temperature by sprinkling a little of the flour/breadcrumb mixture into it. If the breadcrumbs immediately begin to sizzle, it is safe to place the fish in the oil.

9.) Gently lay the fish in the oil. BE VERY CAREFUL! Do not drop the fish in quickly, but be sure not to touch the oil at all, or cause it to splash. If you're uncomfortable using your bare hands, use a pair of metal tongs.

10.) After about three minutes, a crust should form, and you can turn the fish, frying it on the other side as well.

11.) Drain on newspaper and/or paper towels.

Chips:

Ingredients:

6 medium sized potatoes (such as Yukon Gold
or red potatoes), scrubbed and peeled
Sea salt and black pepper
1 tsp. paprika
1 tbsp. olive or grape seed oil

Directions

1.) Peel and slice the potatoes lengthwise, making between four and six pieces for each potato.

2.) Preheat oven to 350°F degrees (175°C).

3.) Blanche potatoes in boiling water for three to four minutes.

4.) Drain, and toss with oil and seasonings.

5.) Spread evenly in a single layer on a baking sheet.

6.) Bake for twenty-thirty minutes, or until crispy.

Shepherd's Pie

Serves 6

Ingredients

1.5 lb (680g) ground beef, turkey, or lamb

1 medium onion, diced

2 cloves garlic, minced

1 tsp. (5mL) black pepper

1 tsp. (5mL) Italian seasoning (or a pinch each of dried oregano, rosemary, and basil)

1 tablespoon (15mL) Worcestershire sauce

2 tbsp. (15g) all-purpose flour

½ cup (120mL) chicken, beef, or vegetable stock.

5 large potatoes, diced and peeled

1 ½ cups (675g) frozen green peas and carrots

3 tbsp. (45g) butter

Salt

Directions

1.) In a medium pot, bring two qt. of water to a boil. Add salt and potatoes. Cook until soft, fifteen-eighteen minutes.

2.) Meanwhile, to a medium skillet, add ground beef, onions, and garlic, cooking until the meat is brown and the onions turn translucent. Add seasonings and Worcestershire sauce.

3.) Stir in flour until well combined. Let cook for about two minutes, until the meat drippings are thick.

4.) Add stock and vegetables; reduce heat to simmer. Cook for approximately five minutes, until thick.

5.) Prepare an oven-safe casserole dish by spraying it with non-stick cooking spray. Carefully place beef mixture in the bottom.

6.) Preheat oven to 350°F (175°C).

7.) Drain potatoes carefully. The water could still be extremely hot!

8.) Using a potato masher or a large spoon, mash the potatoes slightly. You want them to be squished, but still in large pieces.

9.) Spoon the potatoes on top of the beef mixture, covering the meat and vegetables completely.

10.) Divide the butter into small pats and place evenly over the potatoes. Sprinkle with salt and pepper to taste.

11.) Bake in the oven for about twenty five-thirty minutes, or until the potatoes are gold in color and the beef and vegetables are bubbling.

Very Berry Trifle

Serves 6

Ingredients

1 1/2 tbsp. cornstarch

1 1/4 cup (300 ml) milk

2 tbsp. vanilla extract

1/4 cup (25g) Confectioner's (powdered) sugar

2 large egg yolks

1 pt. (225g) strawberries, cleaned and stems removed

½ pt. (150g) raspberries

4 oz. (115g) ready-made pound cake

1 1/4 c (300mL) heavy cream

Directions

1.) Over medium heat, in a small saucepan, mix the cornstarch and a few tablespoons of the milk a whisk until smooth. This is helps you avoid clumps.

2.) Then, slowly add in the rest of the milk and half of the Confectioner's sugar and the vanilla, stirring constantly.

3.) Bring to a boil, while never stopping the stirring. Remove from heat once the mixture is boiling.

4.) Using an electric mixer (or simply a clean whisk) beat the eggs in a bowl, until they are pale yellow in color.

5.) Gradually, while stirring the milk mixture, pour in the eggs. You must remember add a little at a time and to mix constantly, or else your eggs with scramble.

6.) Simmer while stirring for about two minutes or until it has become very thick. Don't boil the custard or else it will curdle.

7.) Remove from heat after it's thick and creamy.

8.) In a blender or food processor puree ¾ c (100g) of strawberries and half the raspberries with the remaining sugar and 4-5 tbsp. of water.

9.) In another bowl stir together the puree and the rest of the berries (save a few for decoration after the trifle is finished).

10.) Cut the pound cake into ¾ in (2cm) squares.

11.) Place the berry puree in a glass serving dish and layer the pound cake on top.

12.) Whip the heavy cream with an electric mixer until stiff peaks form.

13.) Once the custard is cool (you can easily touch the outside of the pot), fold in the whipped cream.

14.) Spoon the custard and cream mixture over the pound cake in an even layer.

15.) Chill for one hour, and then decorate with remaining berries.

Tiramisu

Serves 6

Ingredients

(1) 8-oz (½ lb or 230 g) container of mascarpone

(1) 8-oz (½ lb or 230 g) container of heavy whipping cream

(1) cup (200 g) white sugar

1 ½ cups (12 fl. oz or 360 mL) espresso (or strongly brewed coffee) at room temperature

3 tsp. (15 mL) vanilla extract

(2) 16-oz (2 lb) packages of ladyfingers

unsweetened cocoa powder or nutmeg to top

Directions

1.) Find a large, shallow bowl. In it, mix the coffee, vanilla, and ½ of the sugar.

2.) In a separate large bowl, beat the whipping cream on high with an electric mixer. When peaks begin to form, add the other half of the sugar. (Cream is easiest to whip when it's very cold. So stick it (and the bowl) in the freezer for five-ten minutes before you begin whipping it).

3.) Beat the mascarpone into the whipped cream once you have nice, stiff peaks.

4.) Prepare a 9 x13-inch pan by greasing it slightly with wither butter or cooking spray.

5.) Take one ladyfinger and dip it quickly in the coffee mixture. Don't let it sit. Quickly turn the ladyfinger over, just dampening both sides, then place it in your 9x13 pan. This prevents the bottom layer of your tiramisu from being too soggy. Repeat this, until you have enough damp ladyfingers to cover the bottom of the dish.

6.) Once the first layer is complete, take 1/4 of the mascarpone and whipped cream mixture, and spread a thin layer on top of the lady fingers.

7.) Create another layer of lady fingers with the same method as in step # 5.

8.) Pour the remaining mascarpone mixture on top, spreading it into a thick layer.

9.) Top generously with unsweetened cocoa powder or sprinkle lightly with nutmeg to top.

10.) Cover and refrigerate for at least two hours. Serve and enjoy!

SELECTED RESOURCES BY GORDON RAMSAY

Cookbooks

Ramsay, Gordon. *Gordon Ramsay Makes It Easy*. Hoboken, NJ: John Wiley, 2005.

Ramsay, Gordon. *Gordon Ramsay's Fast Food: More Than 100 Delicious, Super-Fast, and Easy Recipes*. New York: Sterling Epicure, 2012.

Ramsay, Gordon. *Gordon Ramsay's Home Cooking: Everything You Need to Know to Make Fabulous Food*. New York, Grand Central Life & Style, 2013.

Ramsay, Gordon. *Gordon Ramsay's Passion for Flavour*. London: Bounty, 2014.

Website

http://www.gordonramsay.com

Restaurants

Restaurant Gordon Ramsay

Petrus

Bread Street Kitchen

Maze

Gordon Ramsay's Plane Food

Gordon Ramsay Pub & Grill

Gordon Ramsay BurGR

CHRONOLOGY

★

Nov. 8, 1966 — Gordon James Ramsay born in Renfrewshire, Scotland

1982 — Earns spot on the Glasgow Rangers football roster

1985 — Released from the Rangers

1986 — Moves to London

1989 — Begins working for Marco Pierre White at Harvey's

1994 — Becomes head chef at Aubergine

1995 — Earns first Michelin star

1995 — Wins first Catey Award

1996 — Marries Cayetana "Tana" Hutcheson

1997 — Earns second Michelin star at Aubergine

1998 — Opens Gordon Ramsay at Royal Hospital Road

1998 — *Boiling Point* documentary airs in U.K.

1998 — First child, daughter Megan, is born

2000 — First cookbook, *A Passion for Flavour*, is published

2000 — Twins Jack and Holly are born

2001 — Earns three stars at Gordon Ramsay at Royal Hospital Road

2002 — Daughter Matilda is born

2004 — *Ramsay's Kitchen Nightmares* premieres in England

2005 — *The F Word* debuts on C4.

2005 — American version of *Hell's Kitchen* debuts

2006 — Appointed OBE

2007 — *Kitchen Nightmares* debuts in the U. S.

2008 — Forms his own production company, One Potato Two Potato

2010 — Restructures Gordon Ramsay Holdings; founds Kavalake Limited

2014 — Calls it quits for *Kitchen Nightmares* shows in the U.K. and U.S.

2015 — Appears in daughter's new television show, *Mathilda and the Ramsay Bunch*

CHAPTER NOTES
★

Chapter 1: A Spicy Childhood

1. Staff, "The World's Highest Paid Celebrities, 2015 Ranking" *Forbes*, retrieved Aug. 2015. (http://www.forbes.com/profile/gordon-ramsay/?list=celebrities)
2. Staff, "What is Gordon Ramsay's Net Worth," The Motley Fool, retrieved Aug. 2015. (http://www.fool.com/investing/general/2015/07/11/seo-gordon-ramsay-net-worth.aspx)
3. Gordon Ramsay, *Roasting in Hell's Kitchen* (New York: HarperCollins, 2006), p. 8
4. Ibid, p. 21
5. Ibid, p. 14
6. Gemma Mullin, "Cooking is a proper life skill and children should learn to do that rather than worrying about exams, says Gordon Ramsay," *Daily Mail Online*, posted Jan. 2015, retrieved Aug. 2015. (http://www.dailymail.co.uk/news/article-2908430/Gordon-Ramsay-tells-children-cooking-important-exams.html)
7. Ramsay, *Roasting in Hell's Kitchen*, p. 61
8. Nicki Gostin, "Hothead Hits It Big," *Newsweek*, April 18, 2005, p. 12
9. Debra Birnbaum, "Hell Is Other People's Kitchens," *Variety,* Oct. 24, 2014, p. 82.
10. Neil Simpson, *Gordon Ramsay: The Biography* (London: John Blake Publishing, Ltd., 206), p. 28.
11. Ramsay, *Roasting In Hell's Kitchen*, p. 62.
12. Ibid, p. 63.
13. Ibid
14. Simpson, *Gordon Ramsay: The Biography*, p. 29.

Chapter 2: Hungry for Experience

1. Neil Simpson, *Gordon Ramsay: The Biography* (London: John Blake Publishing, Ltd., 206), p. 31.
2. Gordon Ramsay, *Roasting in Hell's Kitchen* (New York: HarperCollins, 2006), p. 64.

3. Debra Birnbaum, "Hell Is Other People's Kitchens," *Variety,* Oct. 24, 2014, p. 82.
4. Ramsay, *Roasting in Hell's Kitchen,* Kindle edition, Chapter 3, location 665.
5. Ibid, location 741.
6. Caroline Frost, "Gordon Ramsay: Chef Terrible," BBC News, posted July 20, 2001, retrieved September 22, 2015, (http://news.bbc.co.uk/2/hi/uk_news/1448742.stm)
7. Bill Buford, "The Taming of the Chef," *The New Yorker,* April 2, 2007, p.
8. Staff writer, "Michel Roux Jr. shares his feelings about Le Gavroche," Big Hospitality, posted April 2007, retrieved Aug. 2015, (http://www.bighospitality.co.uk/People/Michel-Roux-Jr-shares-his-feelings-about-Le-Gavroche)
9. Ramsay, *Roasting in Hell's Kitchen,* Kindle edition, Chapter 4, location 956.

Chapter 3: Calling the Shots

1. Neil Simpson, *Gordon Ramsay: The Biography* (London: John Blake Publishing, Ltd., 206), p. 45.
2. Gordon Ramsay, *Roasting in Hell's Kitchen* (New York: HarperCollins, 2006), Kindle edition, Chapter 7, location 1405.
3. Tom Buerkle, "Chef's Walkout, With Staff, Sets London Abroil," the *New York Times,* July 1998, retrieved Aug. 2015. (http://www.nytimes.com/1998/07/30/style/30iht-lfood.t.html)
4. Moira Hodgson, "London's Tough Chef Ramsay, Serving Up Dainty Delicacies," the *London Observer,* Jan. 1999, retrieved Aug. 2015. (http://observer.com/1999/01/londons-tough-chef-ramsay-serving-up-dainty-delicacies/#ixzz3kE90TpPa)
5. Debra Birnbaum, "Hell Is Other People's Kitchens," *Variety,* Oct. 24, 2014, p. 82.
6. Ramsay, *Roasting in Hell's Kitchen,* Kindle edition, Chapter 9, location 1796.

7. Natasha Stokes, "Best airport restaurants around the world," CNN, posted Oct. 2014, retrieved Sept. 2015. (http://www.cnn.com/2014/04/27/travel/best-airport-restaurants/index.html)

Chapter 4: **Screen and Page**

1. Bill Buford, "The Taming of the Chef," *The New Yorker*, posted April 2007, retrieved June 2015. (http://www.newyorker.com/magazine/2007/04/02/the-taming-of-the-chef)

2. Ibid.

3. Brent Lang, "Gordon Ramsay's Recipe for Anger Management," The Wrap, posted July 2012, retrieved Aug. 2015. (http://www.thewrap.com/gordon-ramsays-recipe-anger-management-45791/)

4. Nicole Lampert, "Without us, you'd still be eating soggy veg: The Roux brothers on how they taught Britain to eat properly," the *Daily Mail*, posted Jan. 2012, retrieved Aug. 2015. (http://www.dailymail.co.uk/femail/article-2088844/The-Roux-Legacy-Without-brothers-Britain-eating-soggy-veg.html)

5. Nancy Banks-Smith, "Learning to Fry," the *Guardian*, posted Nov. 2001, retrieved Aug. 2015.(http://www.theguardian.com/media/2001/nov/07/tvandradio.television1)

6. Gordon Ramsay, *Roasting in Hell's Kitchen* (New York: HarperCollins, 2006), Kindle edition, Chapter 12, location 2551.

7. Tom Peterkin, "Gordon Ramsay Nearly Dies After Cliff Fall," *The (London) Telegraph*, posted July 2008, retrieved Aug. 2015. (http://www.telegraph.co.uk/news/celebritynews/2464417/Gordon-Ramsay-nearly-dies-after-cliff-fall.html)

8. Decca Aitkenhead, "Gordon Ramsay: appetite for destruction," *The Guardian*, posted June 2012, retrieved Aug. 2015. (http://www.theguardian.com/lifeandstyle/2012/jun/08/gordon-ramsay-behind-bars)

9. Cole Moreton, "'The kids know the fame is a result of hard work': Gordon Ramsay on swearing, feuds with other chefs and how his 13-year-old daughter landed her own cooking show," Mail Online, posted April 2015, retrieved Aug. 2015. (http://www.

dailymail.co.uk/home/event/article-3032351/Gordon-Ramsay-teenage-daughter-s-cooking-swearing-feuds-chefs.html)

10. Ramsay, *Roasting in Hell's Kitchen*, Chapter 12, location 2580.

11. Kate O'Hare, "'Hell's Kitchen' and 'Masterchef's' Gordon Ramsay: 'Have you any idea how competitive dinner parties have become?'" Zap2it, posted June 2012, retrieved Aug. 2015. (http://zap2it.com/blog-post/hells-kitchen-and-masterchefs-gordon-ramsay-have-you-any-idea-how-competitive-dinner-parties-have-become/)

12. Leora Arnowitz, "Gordon Ramsay gets sensitive on 'MasterChef Junior,'" Fox 411, posted Jan. 2015, retrieved Sept. 2015. (http://www.foxnews.com/entertainment/2015/01/20/gordon-ramsay-gets-sensitive-on-masterchef-junior/)

13. Andrew Pierce, "Gordon Ramsay: The F Factor," *The (London) Telegraph*, posted Oct. 2008, retrieved Aug. 2015. (http://www.telegraph.co.uk/foodanddrink/3345890/Gordon-Ramsay-the-F-Factor.html)

14. Ramsay, *Roasting in Hell's Kitchen*, Chapter 12, location 2580.

Chapter 5: **Beyond the Kitchen**

1. Andrew Pierce, "Gordon Ramsay: The F Factor," *The (London) Telegraph*, posted Oct. 2008, retrieved Aug. 2015. (http://www.telegraph.co.uk/foodanddrink/3345890/Gordon-Ramsay-the-F-Factor.html)

2. Ibid

3. Staff reporter, "Gordon Ramsay forced to give up flagship U.S. restaurant despite massive cutbacks," *The Daily Mail*, posted Dec. 2009, retrieved Sept. 2015. (http://www.dailymail.co.uk/tvshowbiz/article-1232986/Gordon-Ramsay-sheds-final-U-S-restaurant-financial-troubles-continue.html)

4. Mark Sweney, "All3Media finalises £40m acquisition of production company Optomen," *The Guardian*, posted Aug. 2010, retrieved Aug. 2015. (http://www.theguardian.com/media/2010/aug/13/all3media-optomen-gordon-ramsay)

5. Nick Allen, "Gordon Ramsay to open cooking academy," *The (London) Telegraph*, posted Oct. 2008, retrieved Aug. 2015. (http://www.telegraph.co.uk/news/celebritynews/3228472/Gordon-Ramsay-to-open-cooking-academy.html)

6. Gordon Ramsay, *Roasting in Hell's Kitchen* (New York: HarperCollins, 2006), Kindle edition, Chapter 12, location 2580.

7. Debra Birnbaum, "Hell Is Other People's Kitchens," *Variety,* Oct. 24, 2014, p. 82.

Chapter 6: **Awards and Honors**

1. Elaina Plott, "Perennial Angry Man Gordon Ramsay Cried Over NYC Michelin Downgrade," *The (London) Observer*, posted Feb. 2014, retrieved Aug. 2015. (http://observer.com/2014/02/perennial-angry-man-gordon-ramsay-cried-over-nyc-michelin-downgrade/)

2. Staff, "Gordon Ramsay," *The Caterer*, posted Sept. 2006, retrieved Sept. 2015. (https://www.thecaterer.com/articles/308871)

3. Ibid

4. Janet Harmer, "Star qualities," *The Caterer*, posted Jan. 2003, retrieved Sept. 2015. (https://www.thecaterer.com/articles/320716/star-qualities)

5. Brent Lang, "Gordon Ramsay's Recipe for Anger Management" *The Wrap*, posted July 2012, retrieved Aug. 2015. (http://www.thewrap.com/gordon-ramsays-recipe-anger-management-45791/)

6. Yelena Moroz Alpert, "12 Celebrities Who Have Run Marathons," *Men's Fitness*, retrieved Sept. 2015. (http://www.mensfitness.com/training/endurance/12-celebrities-who-have-run-marathons/slide/10

7. Staff, "Gordon Ramsay and Scottish celebrities support charity fundriaser," *Faces of Spina Bifida Magazine*, posted May 2012, retrieved Sept. 2015. (http://facesofspinabifida.com/articles/gordon-ramsay-and-scottish-celebrities-support-charity-fundraiser)

8. Staff, "Ramsay opens spina bifida centre," BBC News, posted Nov. 2006, retrieved Sept. 2015. (http://news.bbc.co.uk/2/hi/uk_news/scotland/glasgow_and_west/6172502.stm)

9. Abram Brown, "Gordon Ramsay's Dream Retirement Project: A Virgin Islands Restaurant Open One Day a Week," posted June 2015, retrieved Sept. 2015. (http://www.forbes.com/sites/abrambrown/2015/06/29/gordon-ramsays-dream-retirement-project-a-virgin-islands-restaurant-open-one-day-a-week/)

Chapter 7: Following in Gordon's Footsteps

1. Staff, "Life of a Sous Chef," Culinary Schools.org, retrieved Sept. 2015. (http://www.culinaryschools.org/chef-types/sous-chef/)

2. Gordon Ramsay. BrainyQuote.com, Xplore Inc, 2015. http://www.brainyquote.com/quotes/quotes/g/gordonrams455568.html, accessed September 22, 2015.

amateur—A person who does something at a lesser skill level than a professional.

apprenticeship—A period of time when a person learns work skills while on the job.

aspiring—Someone who wants to achieve a certain level of success.

celebrated—A person who is well known and praised for something they have accomplished

certification—An official, usually written approval that someone has reached a certain skill or knowledge level.

chopping—The act of cutting up food roughly into pieces.

commuting—Traveling regularly between locations.

culinary—Of or relating to cooking.

dice—To cut up food into small cubes.

endorsement—A public statement of support or approval.

finesse—Skill or cleverness at a task.

gourmet—Fancy, special, or elaborate, with regard to food.

internship—A temporary employment situation with an emphasis on learning job skills.

licensing agreement—A contract that gives a business the right to use another business's name or ideas.

mince—To cut food into pieces that are very small.

mis en place—A French term meaning "everything in its place."

slouch—Someone who is lazy or not very useful.

subsidiary—Owned or controlled by another; lesser than.

FURTHER READING

Books

Culinary Institute of America, *The Professional Chef.* Hoboken, NJ: John Wiley & Sons, 2011.

Gibney, Michael. *Sous Chef: 24 Hours On the Line.* New York, NY: Ballantine Books, 2015.

Gregory, Jeff. *Cool Careers: Chef.* North Mankato, MN: Cherry Lake Publishing, 2014.

Meyer, Susan. *A Career As a Chef.* New York, NY: Rosen Publishing, 2012.

Websites

gordonramsay.com
Gordon Ramsay's official website

bbcgoodfood.com/recipes/collection/gordon-ramsay
A treasure trove of some of Ramsay's great recipes

fox.com/masterchef
The official site for Ramsay's intense television show

INDEX

⭐